BIBLICAL LANDSCAPES COLORING BOOK

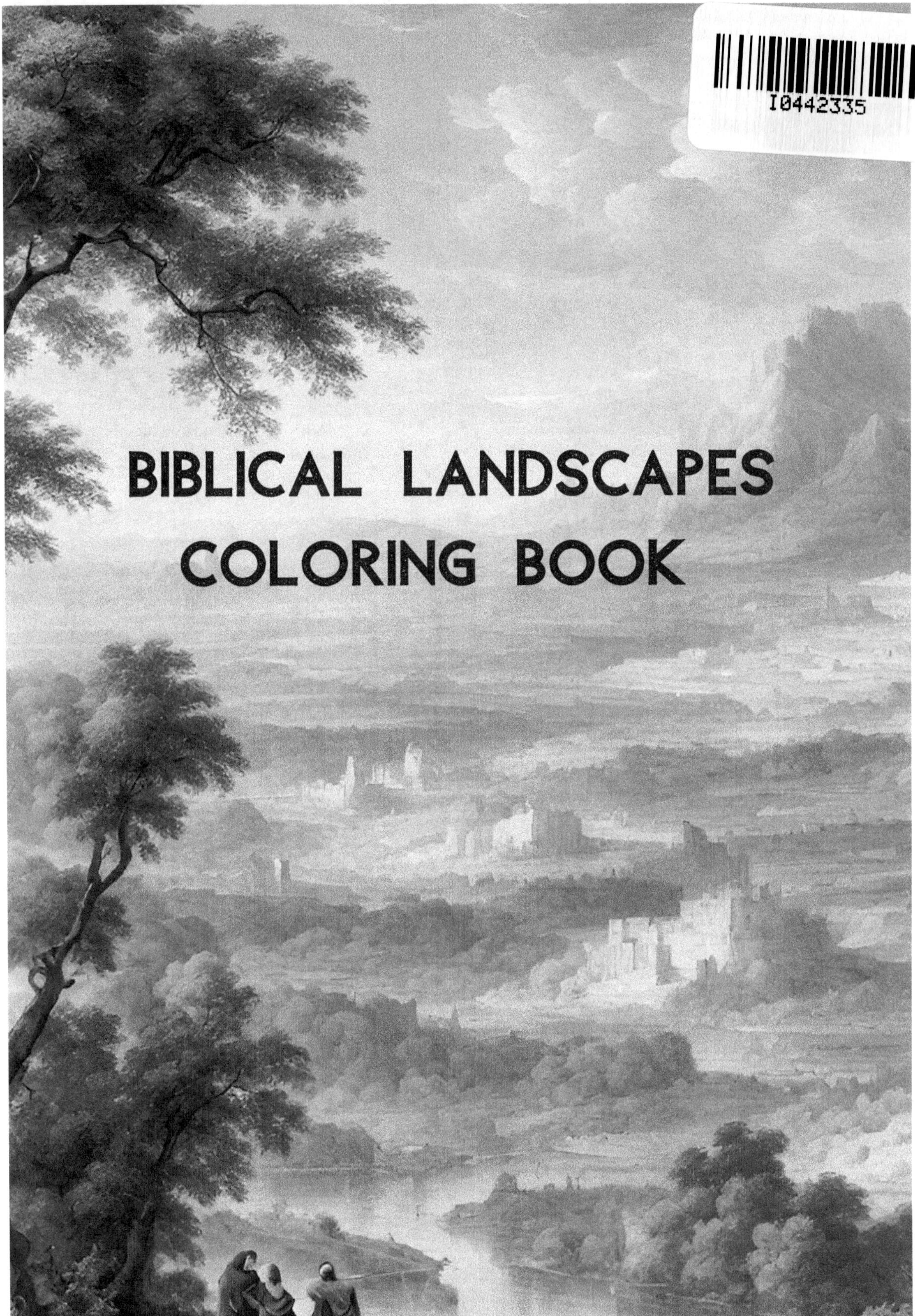

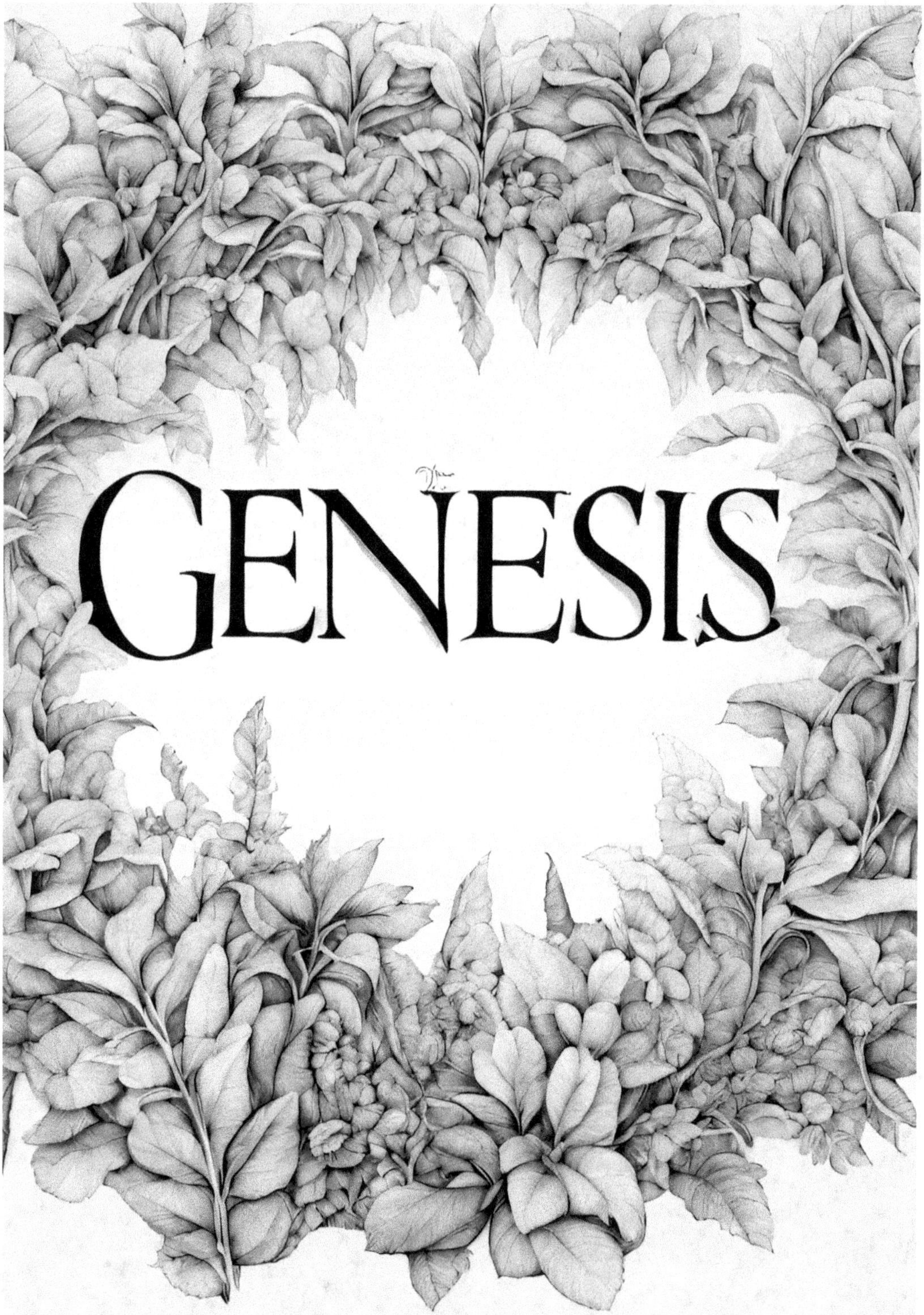
GENESIS

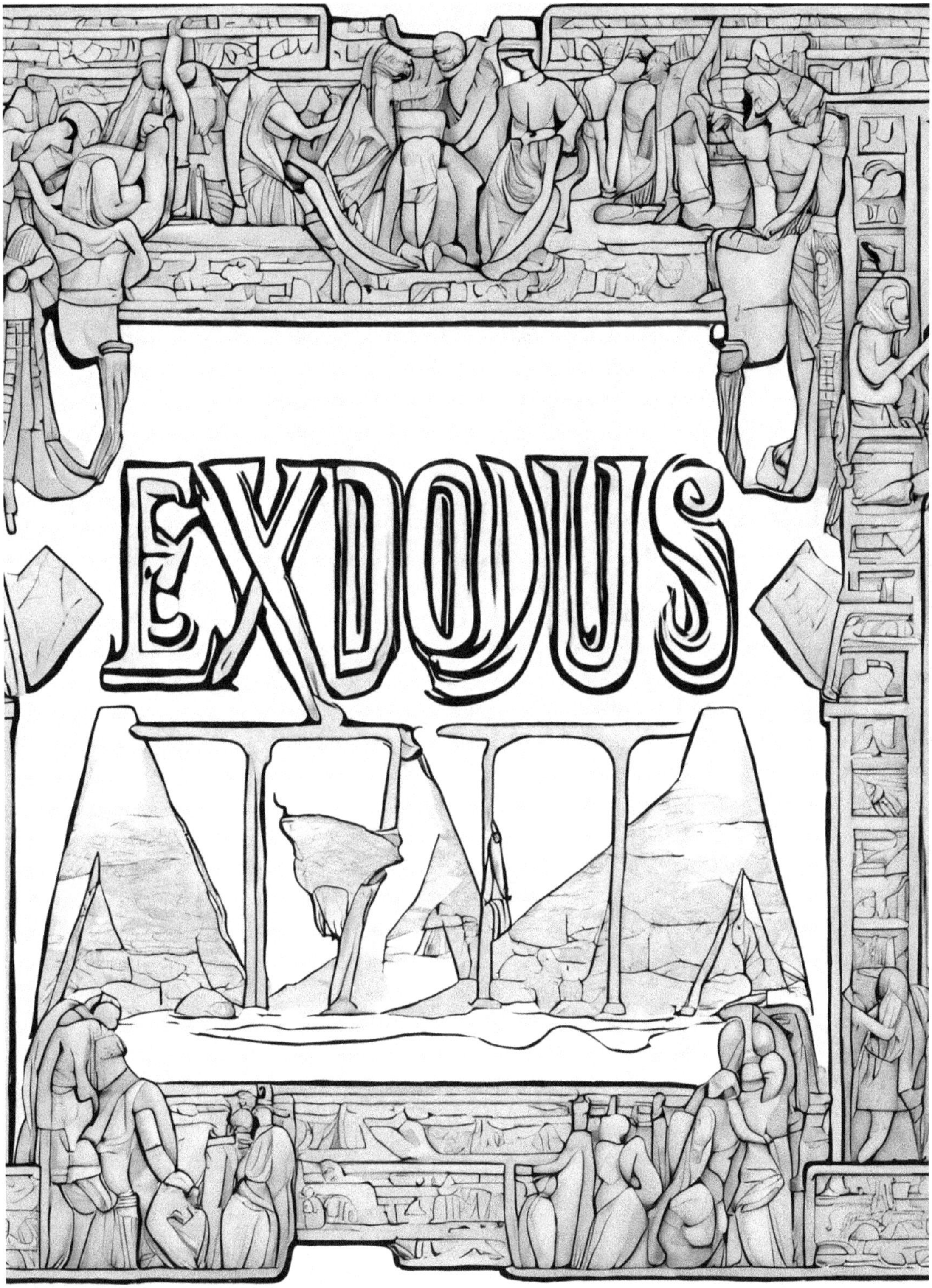
EXDOUS

LEVITICUS

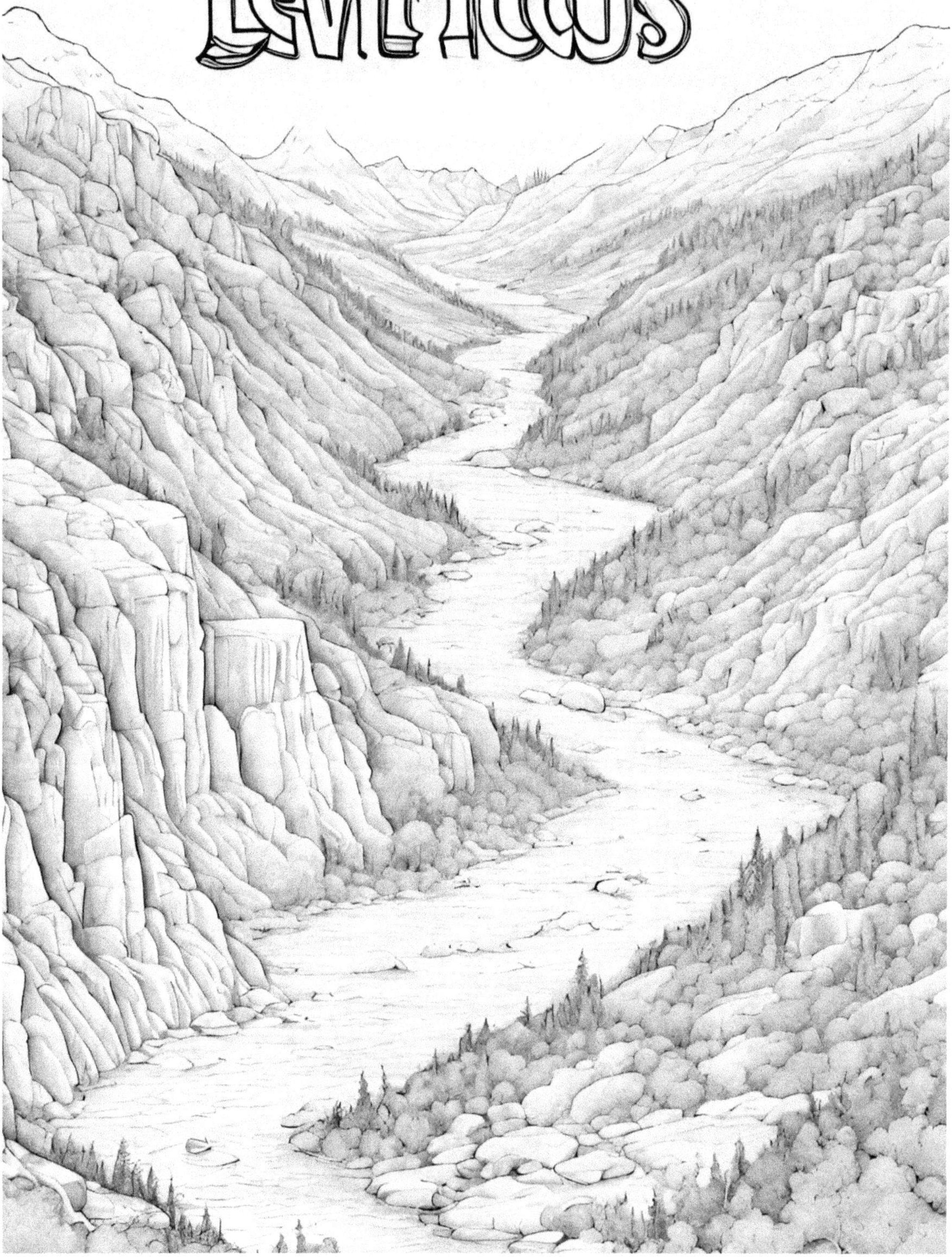

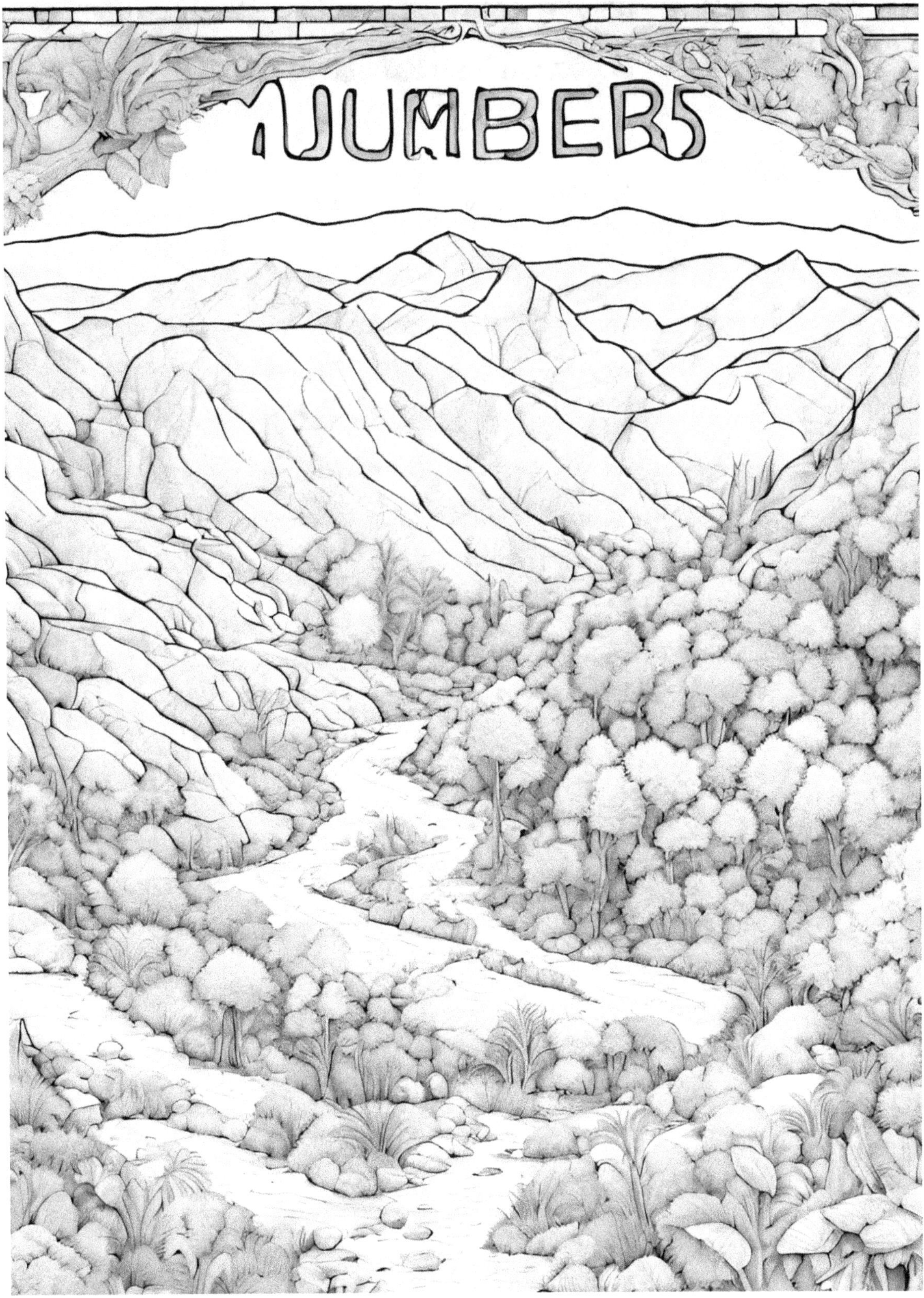
NUMBERS

DEUTERONOMY

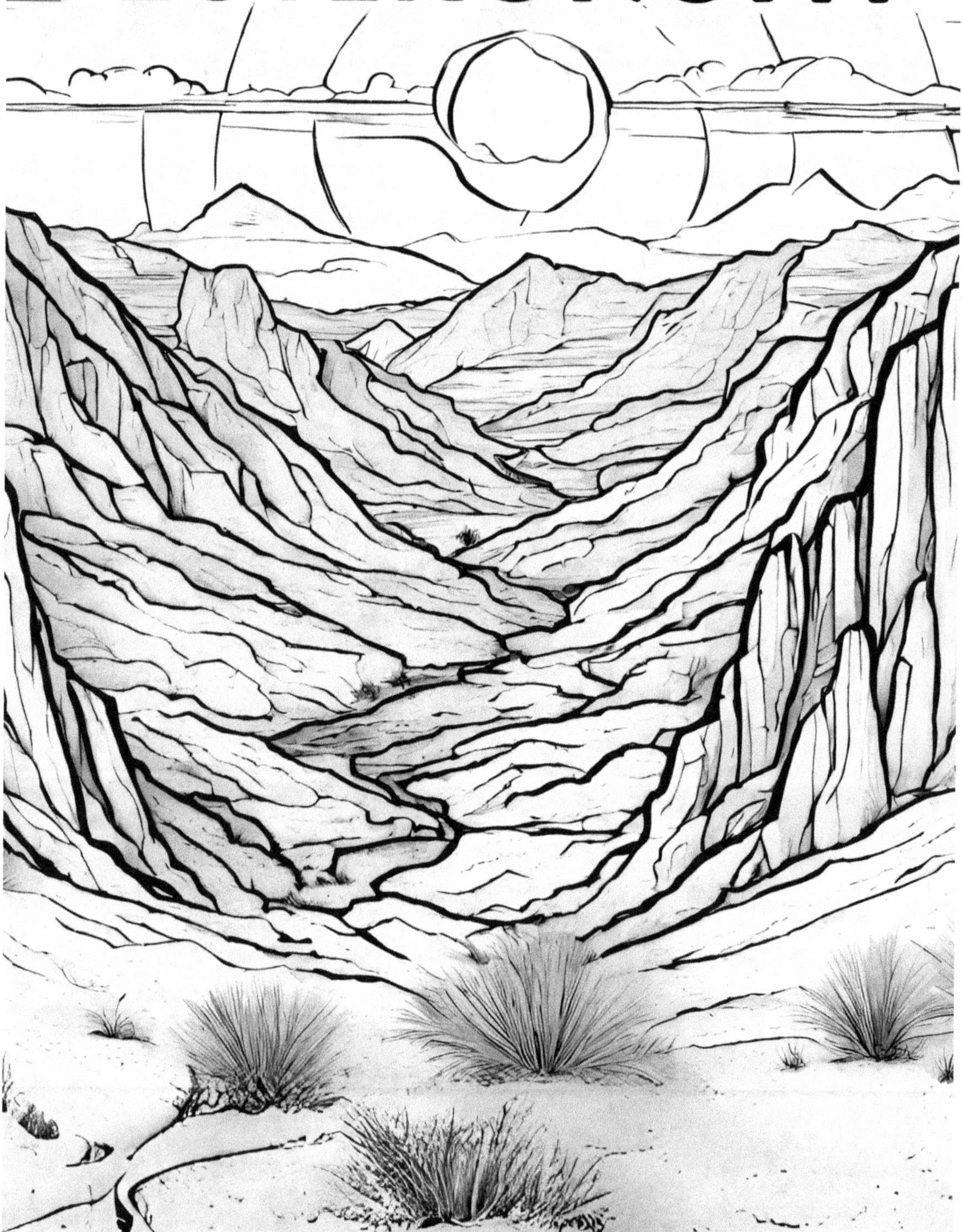

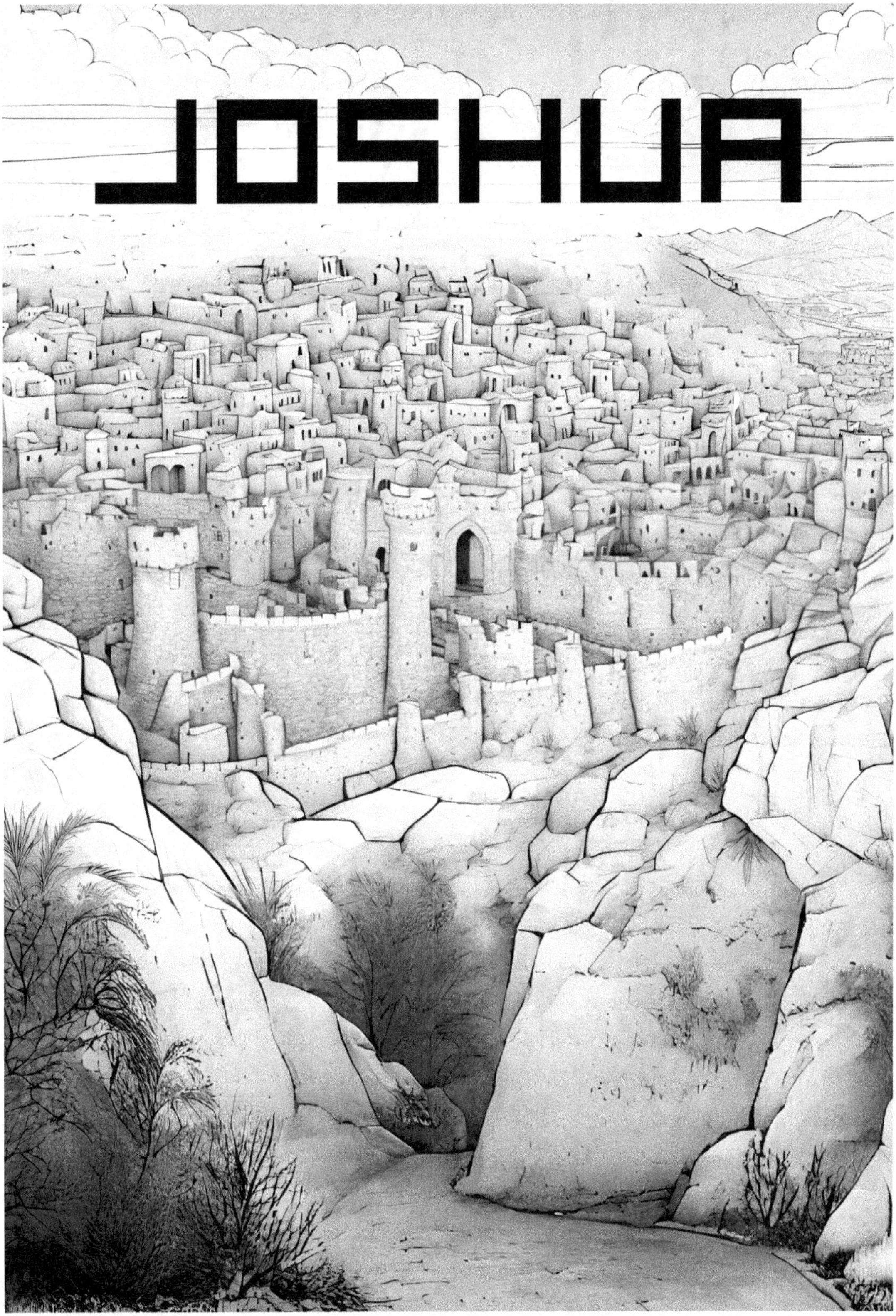
JOSHUA

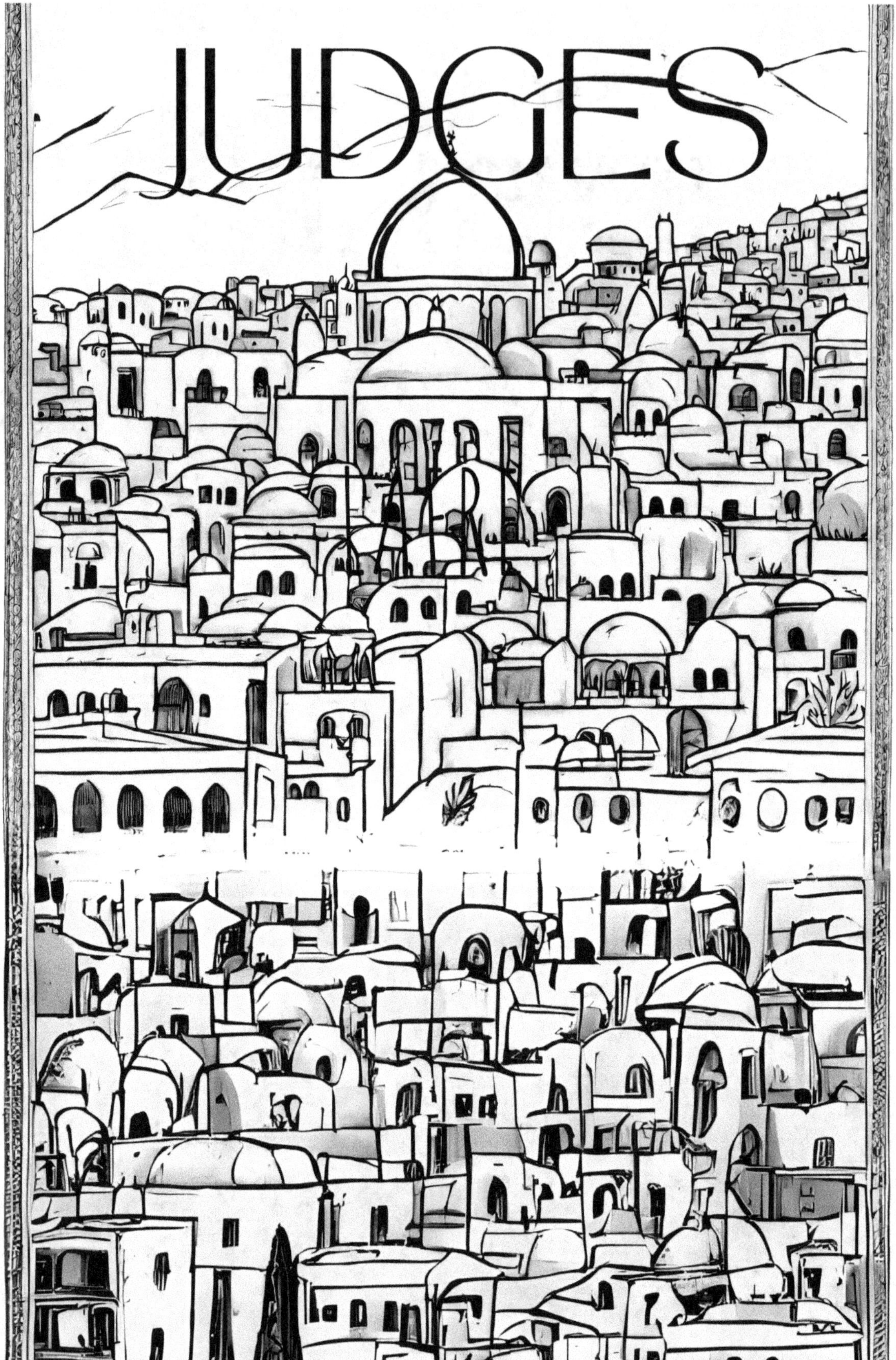
JUDGES

RUTH

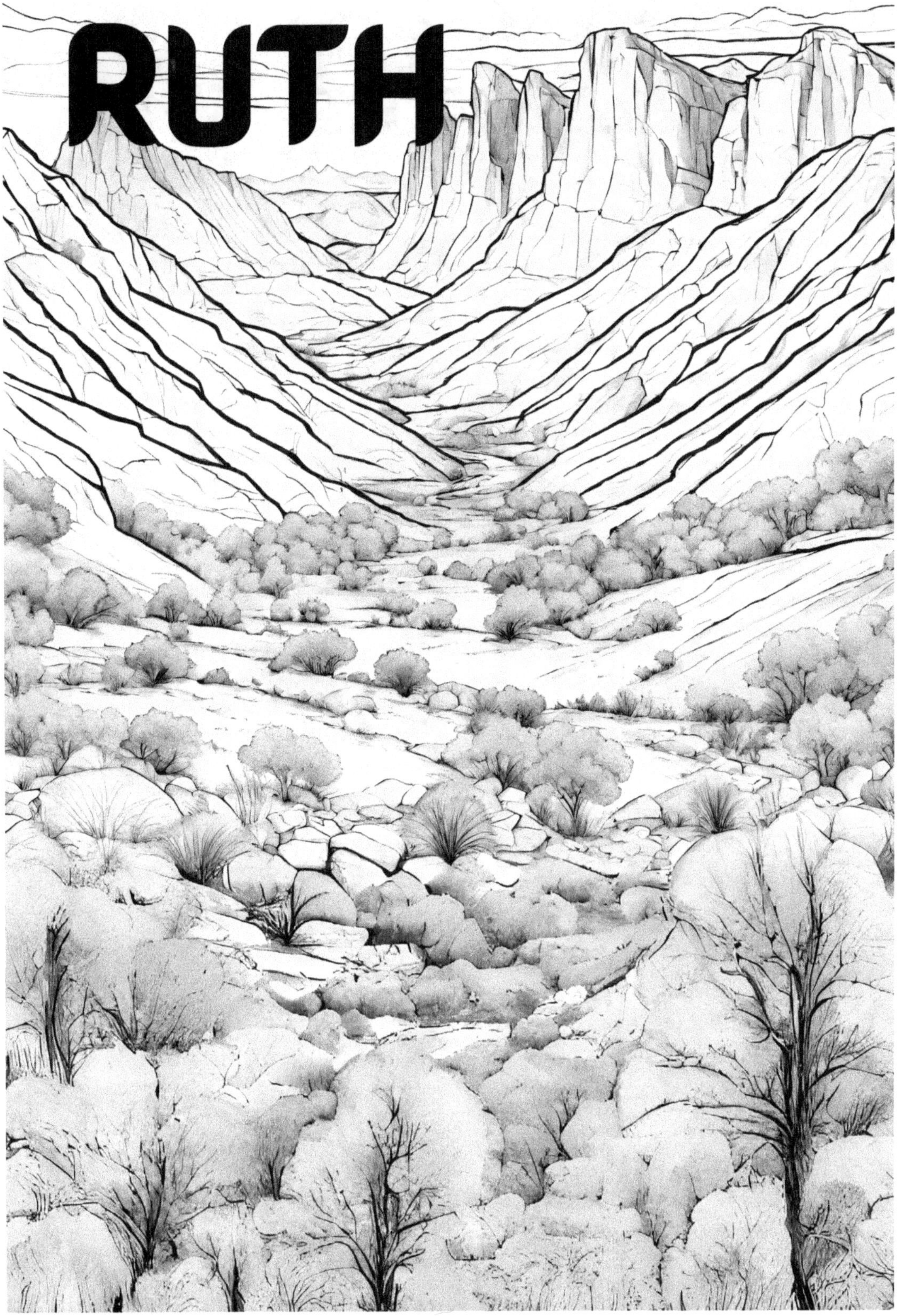

1ST & 2ND SAMUEL

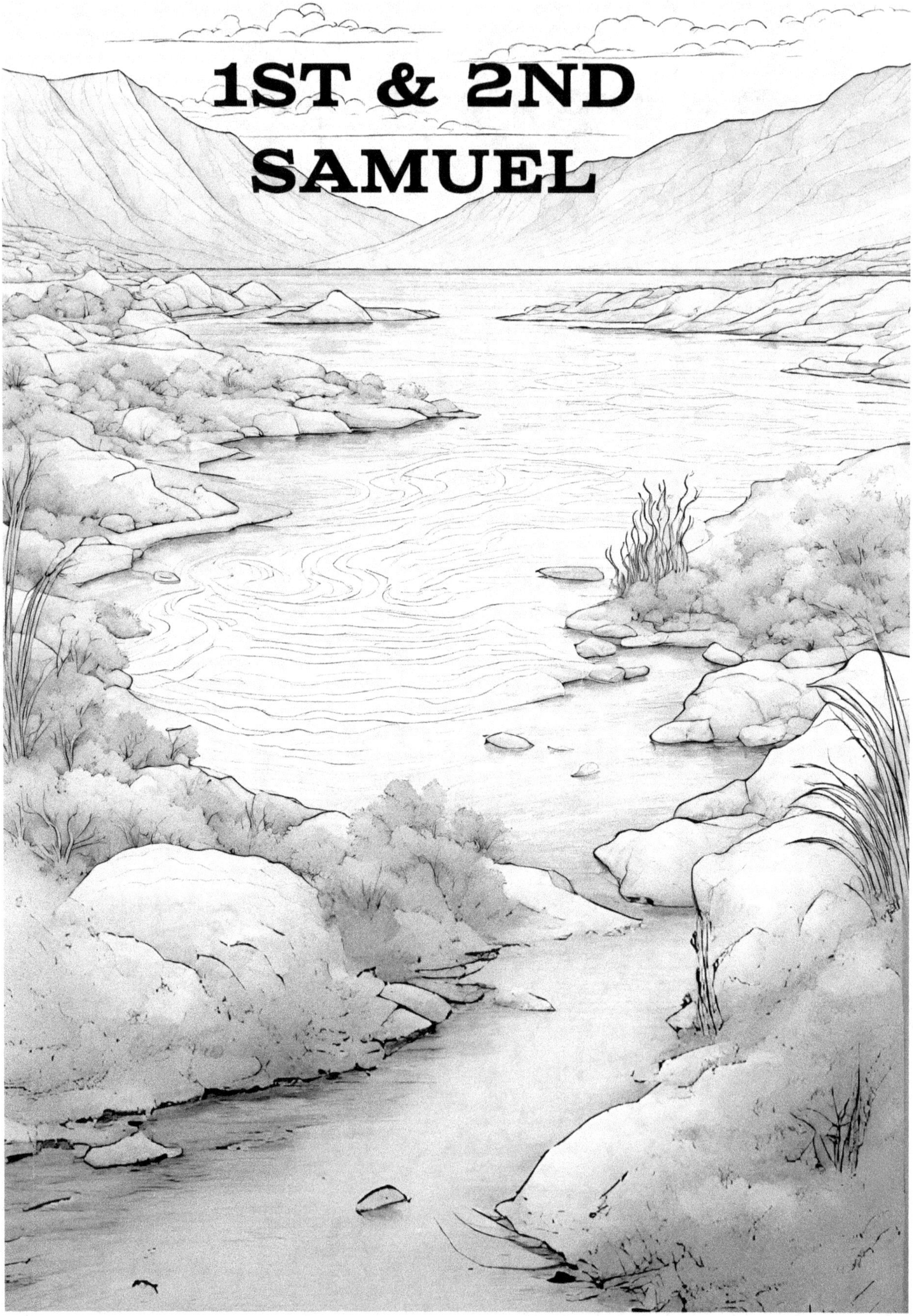

1st & 2nd Kings

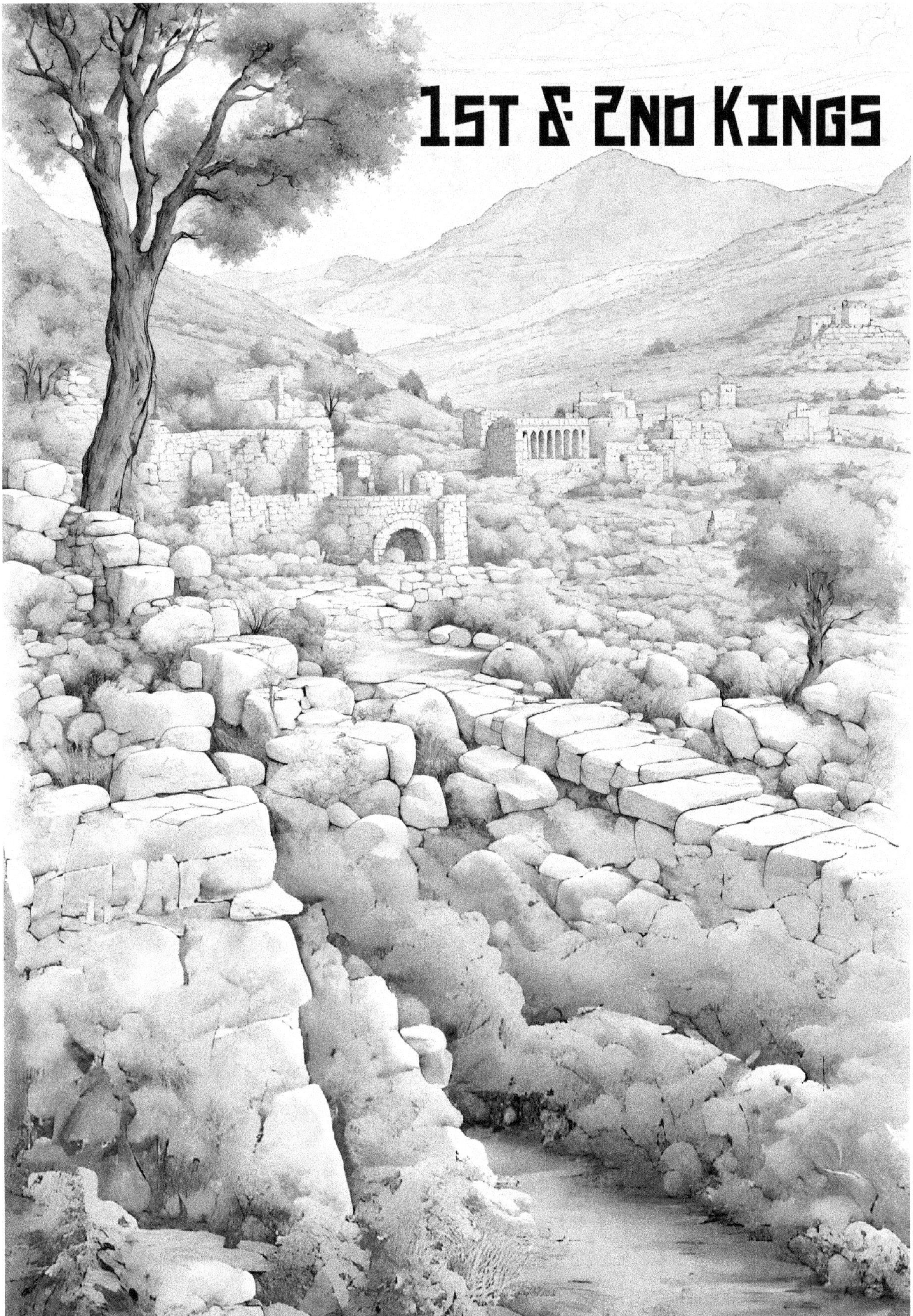

1st & 2nd Chronicles

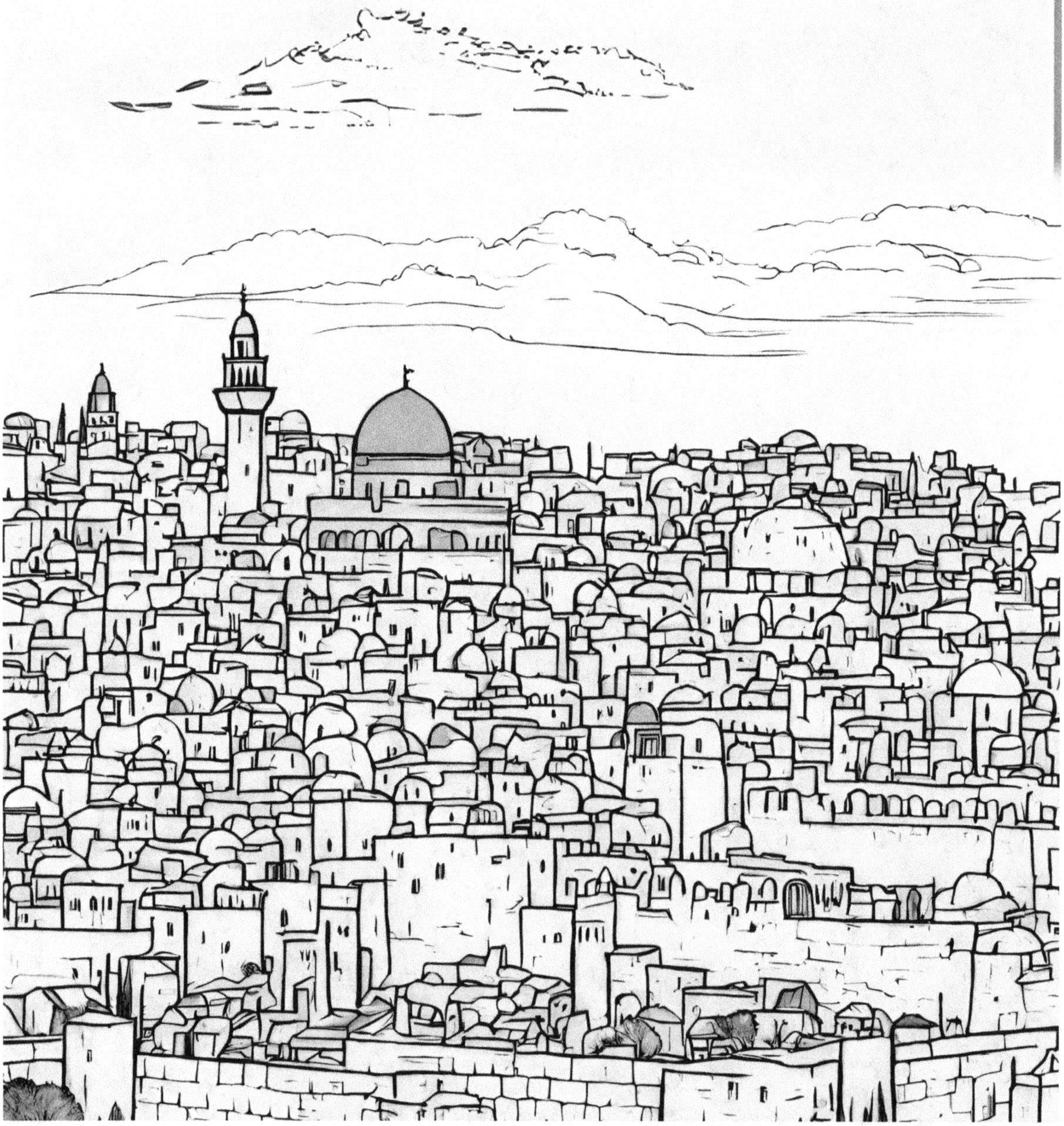

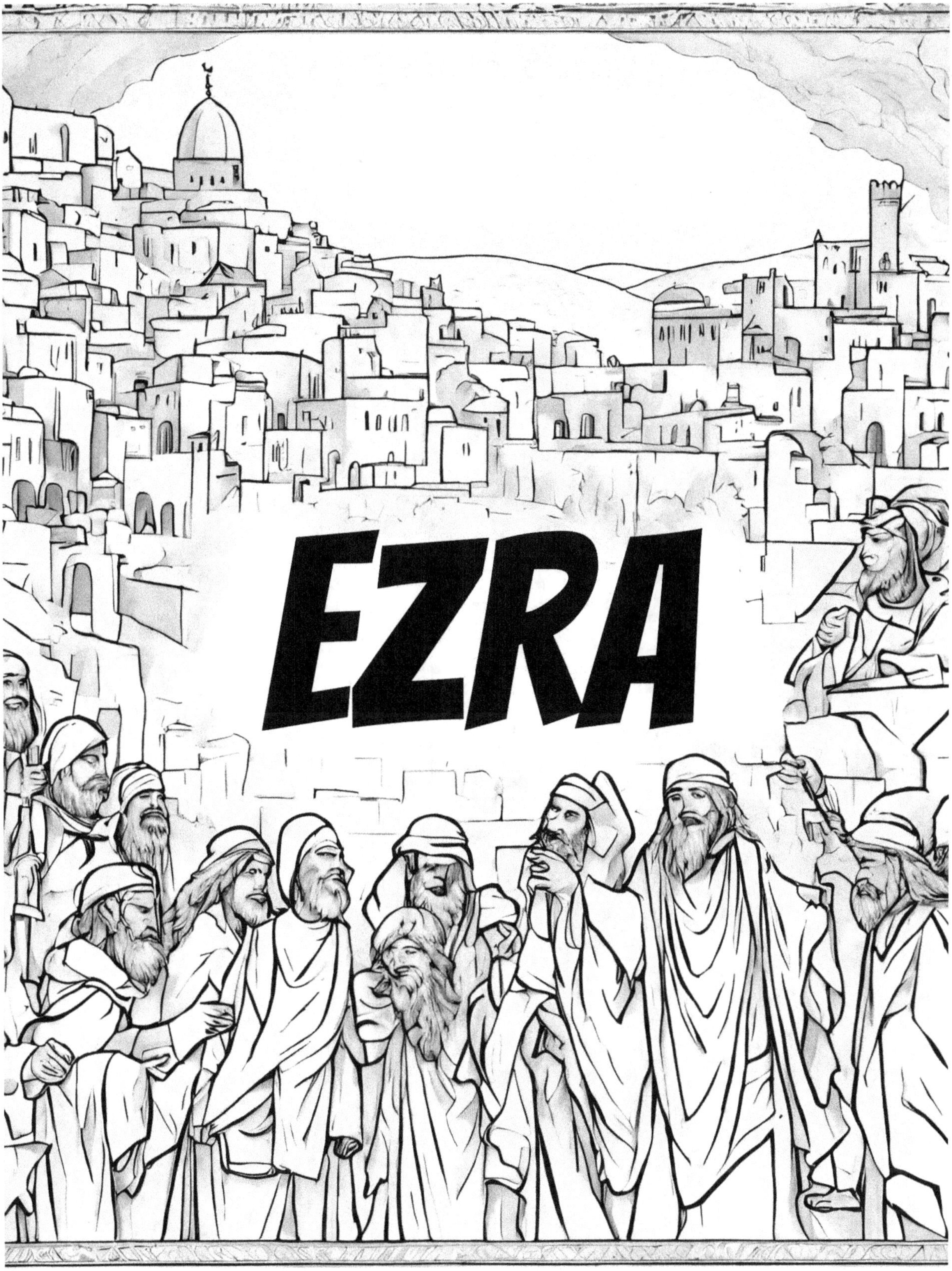
EZRA

Nehemiah

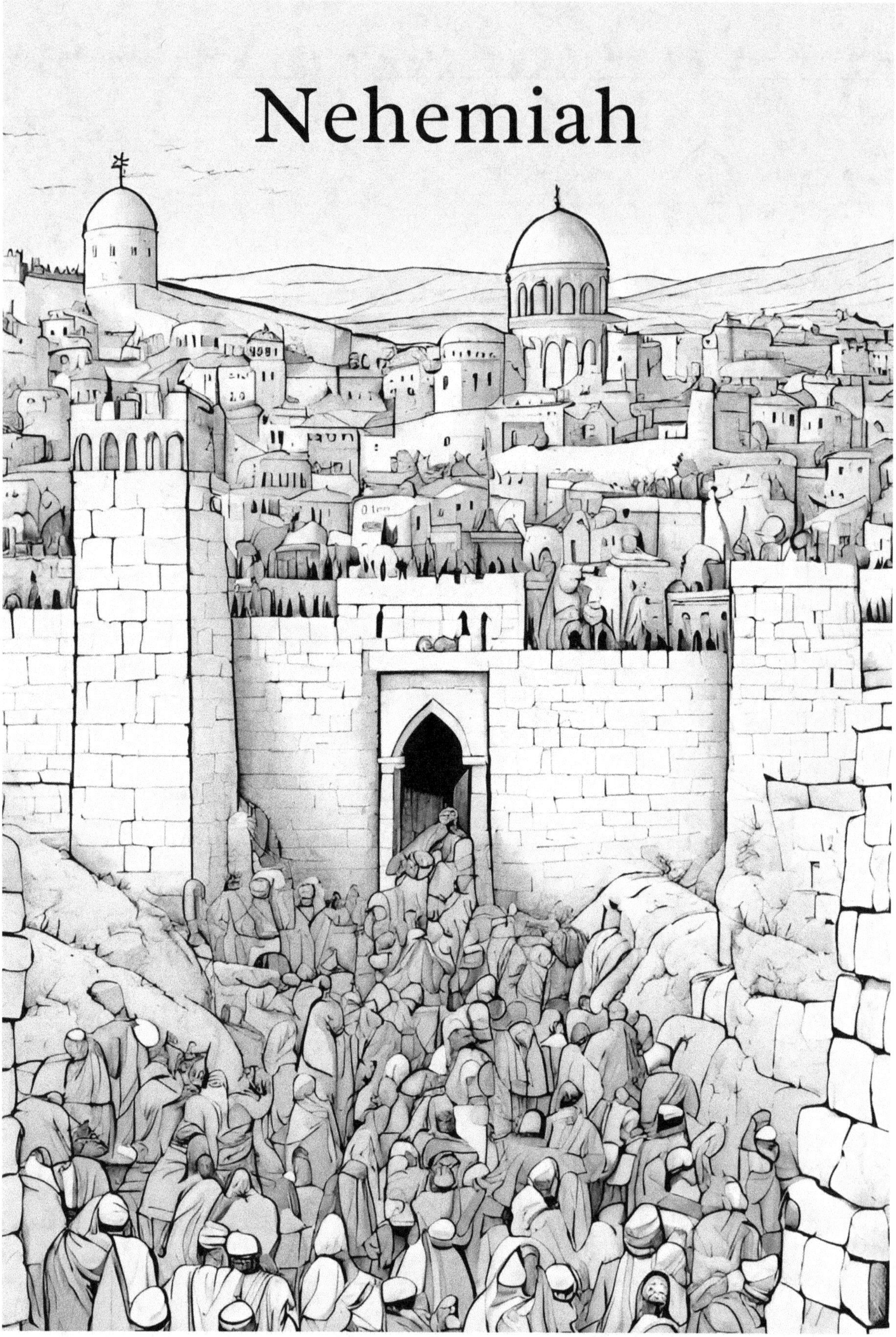

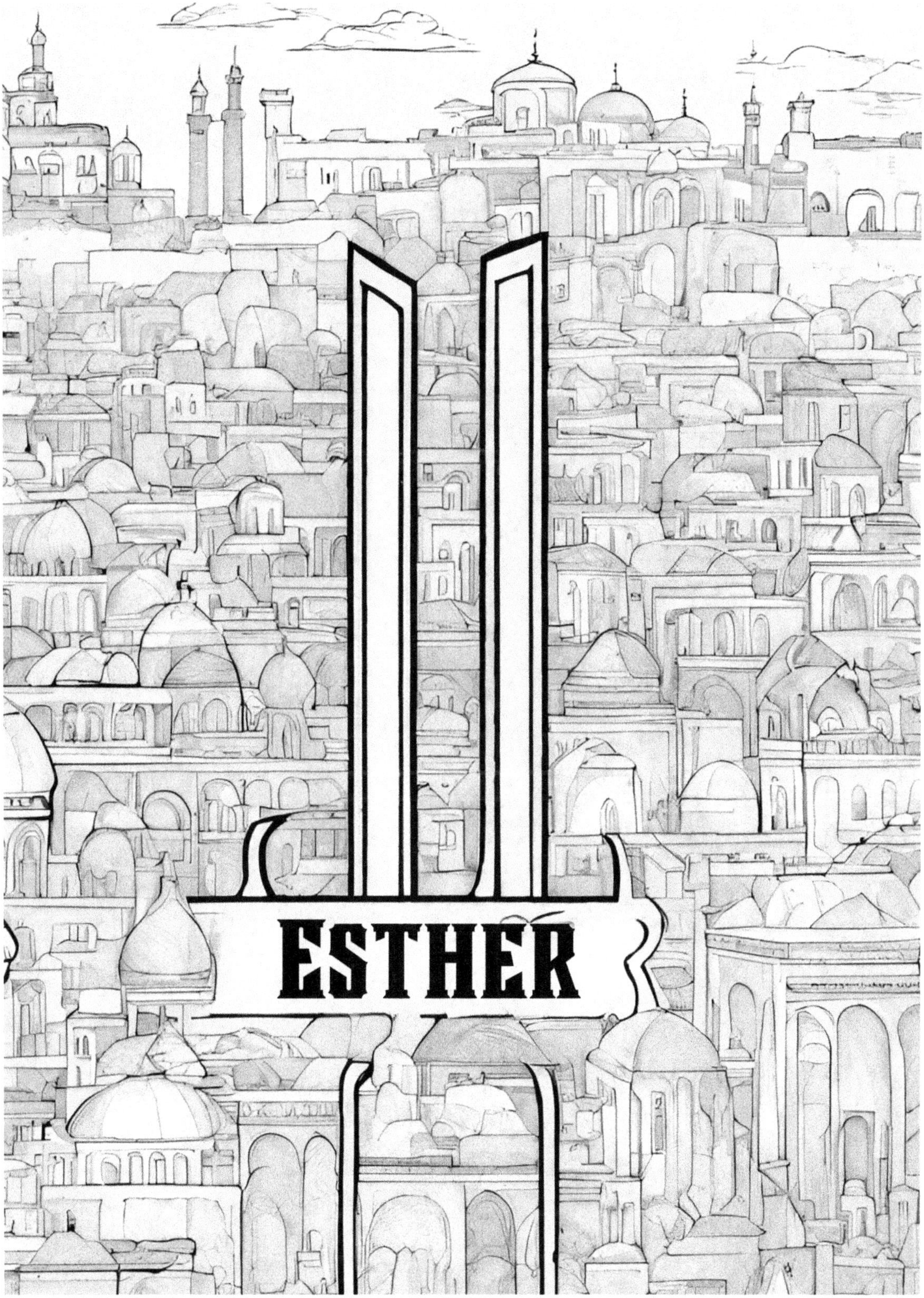
ESTHER

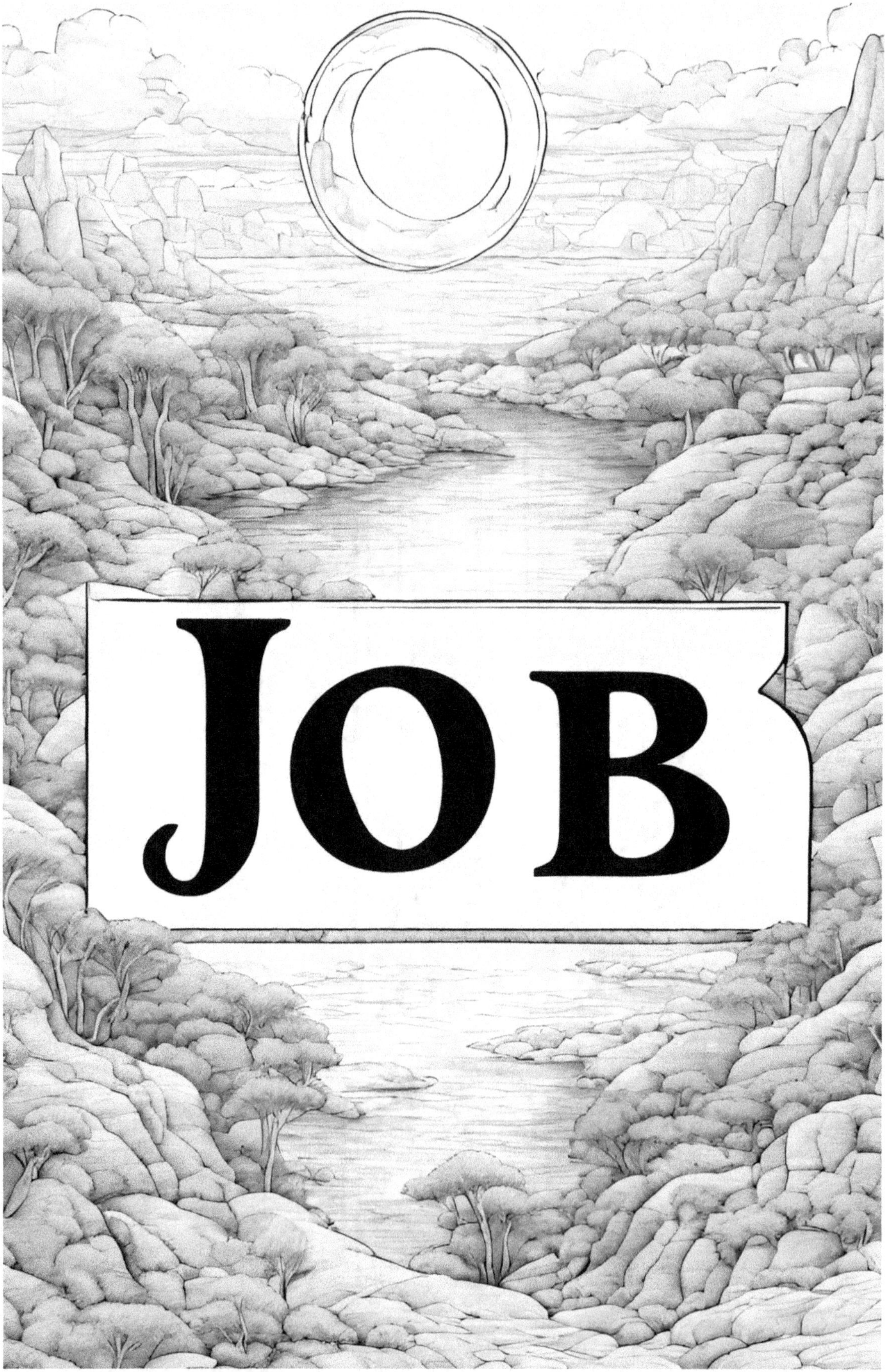
JOB

Psalms

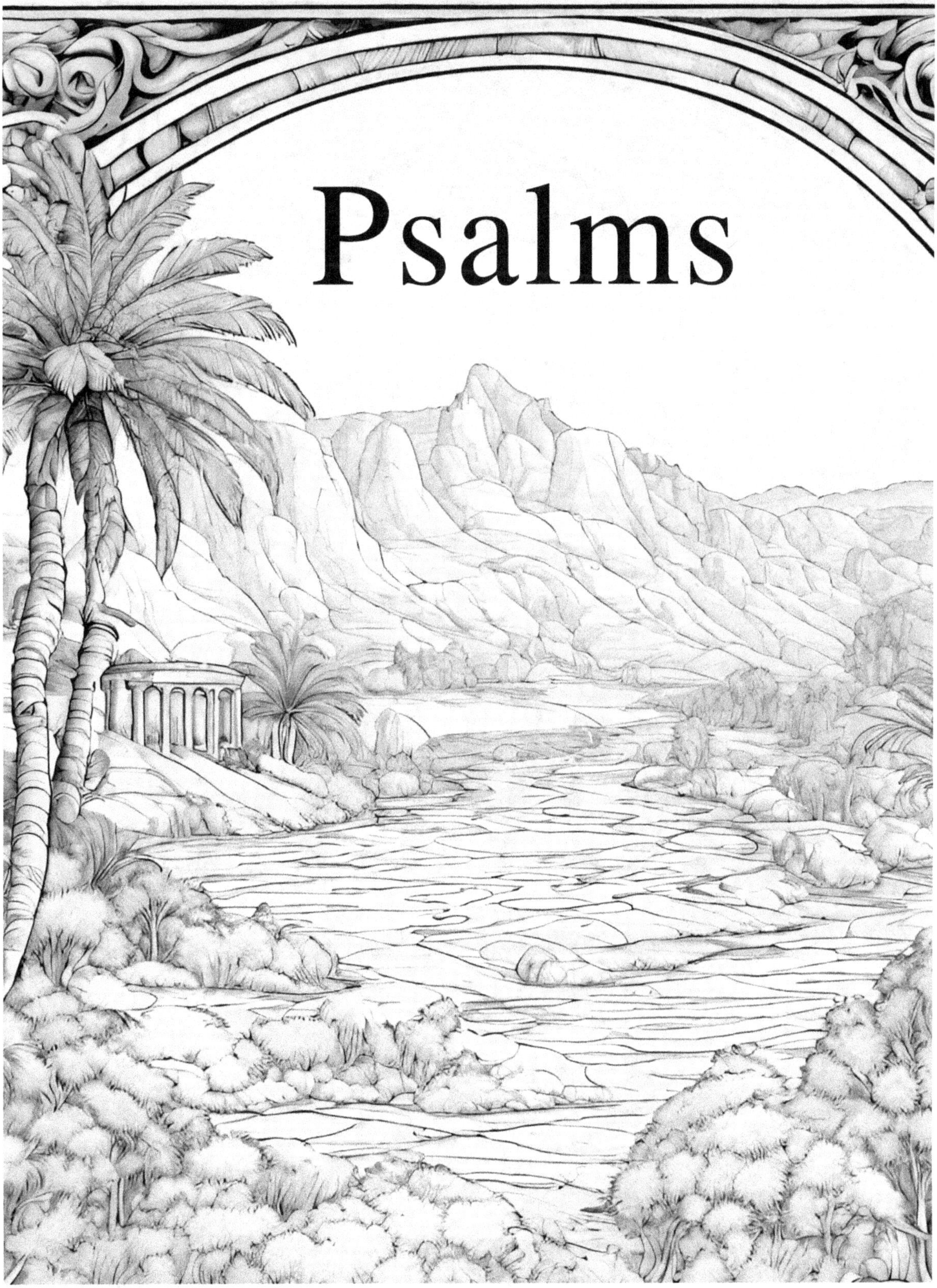

PROVERBS

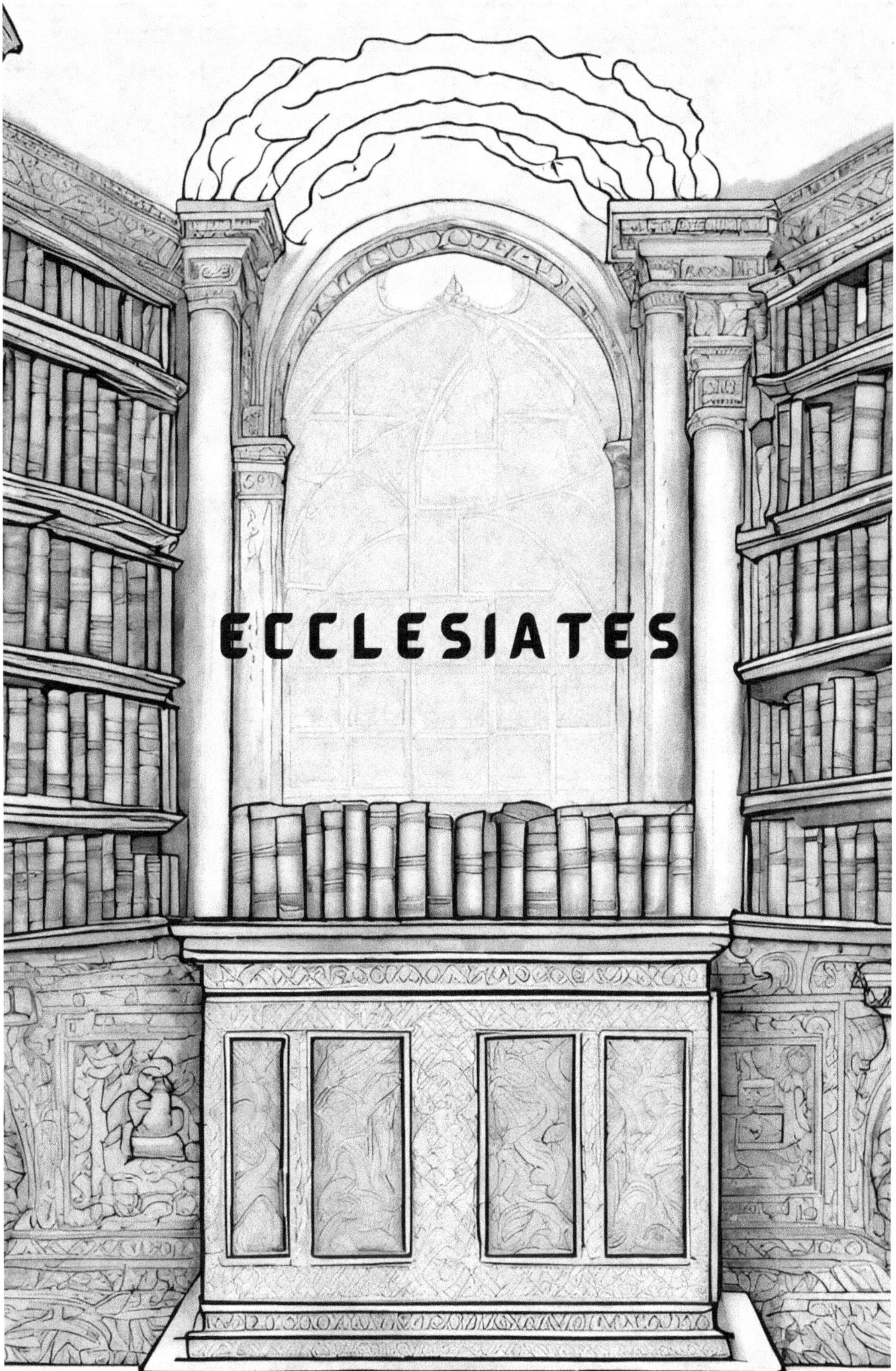
ECCLESIATES

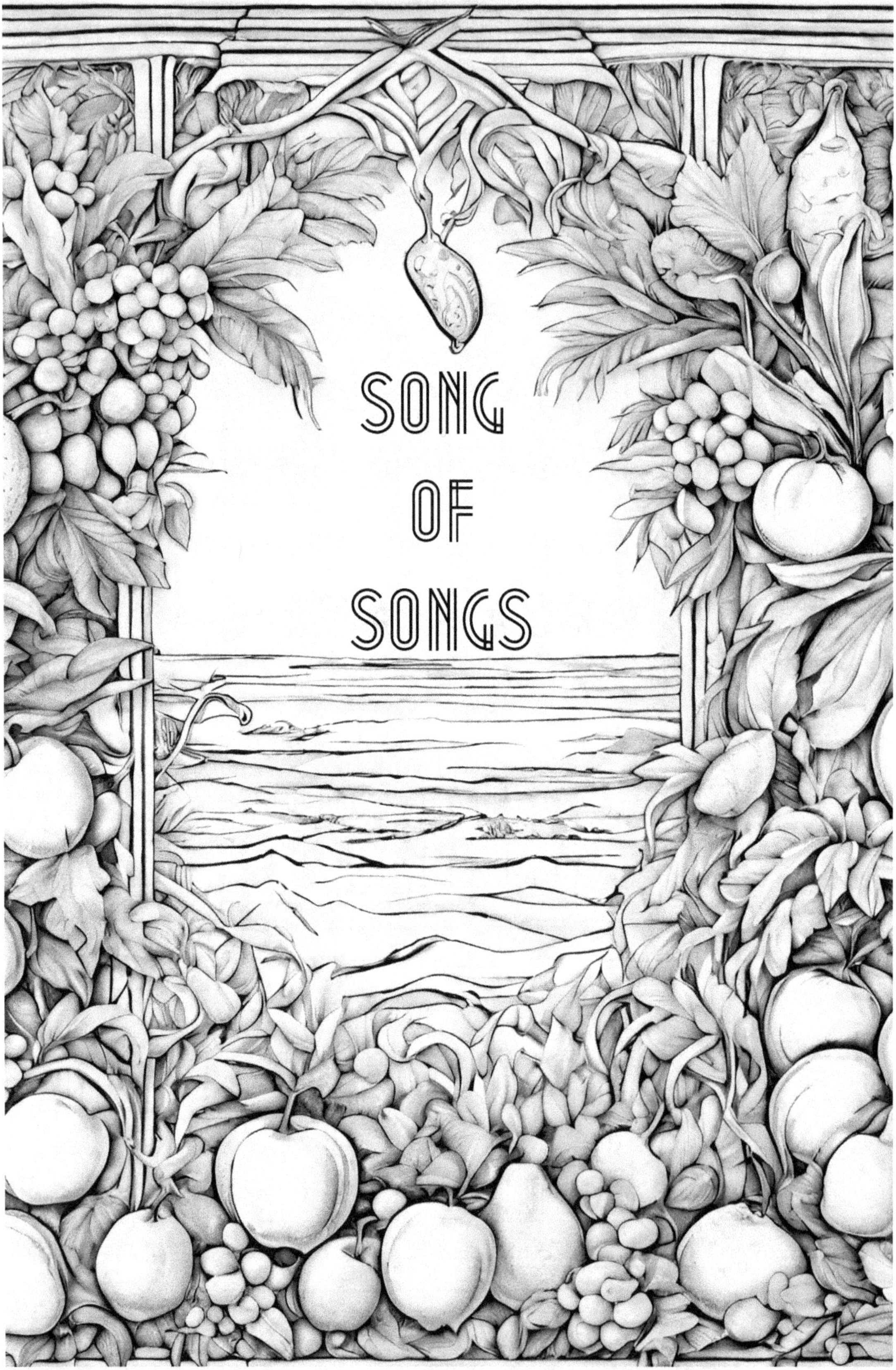
SONG
OF
SONGS

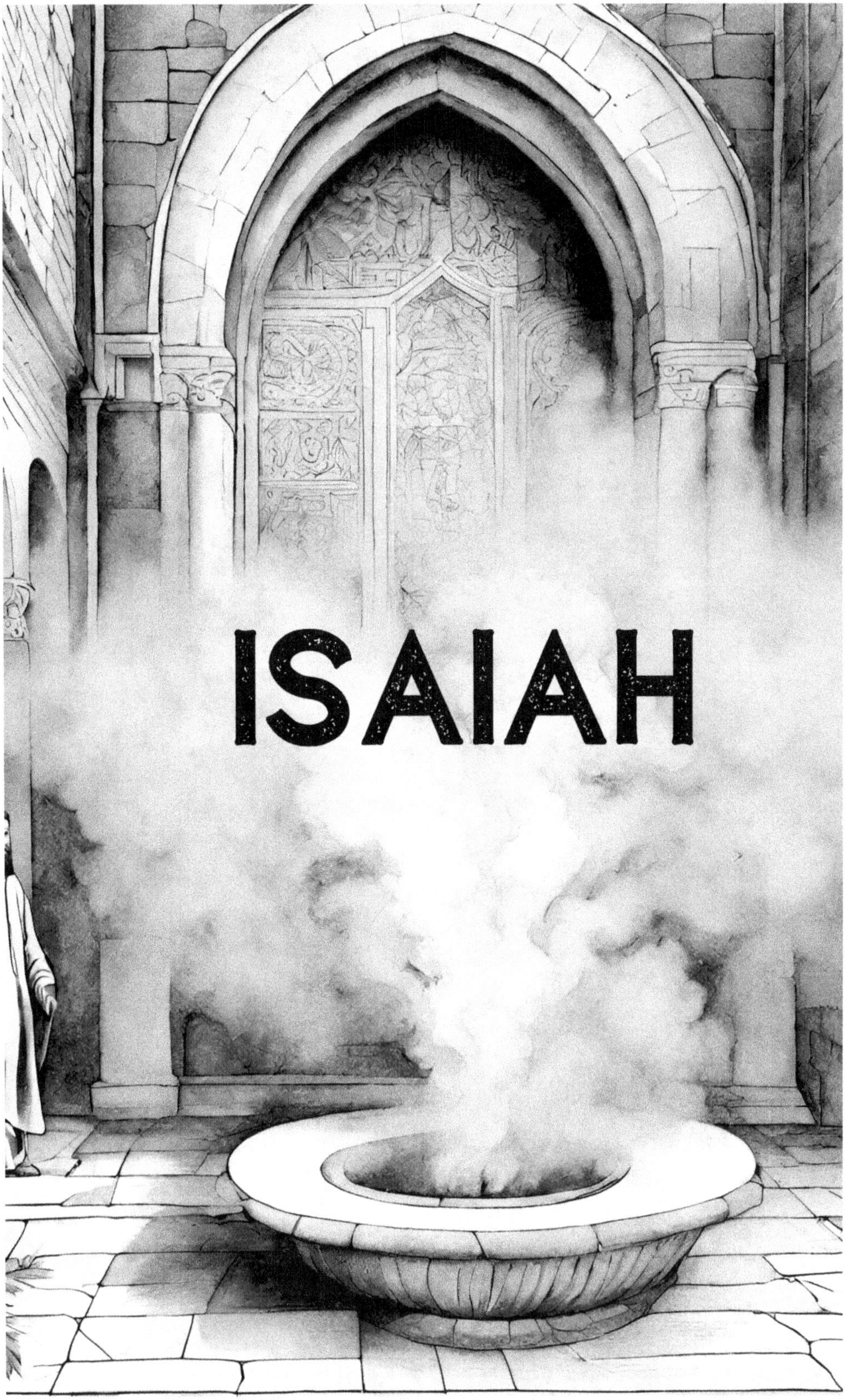
ISAIAH

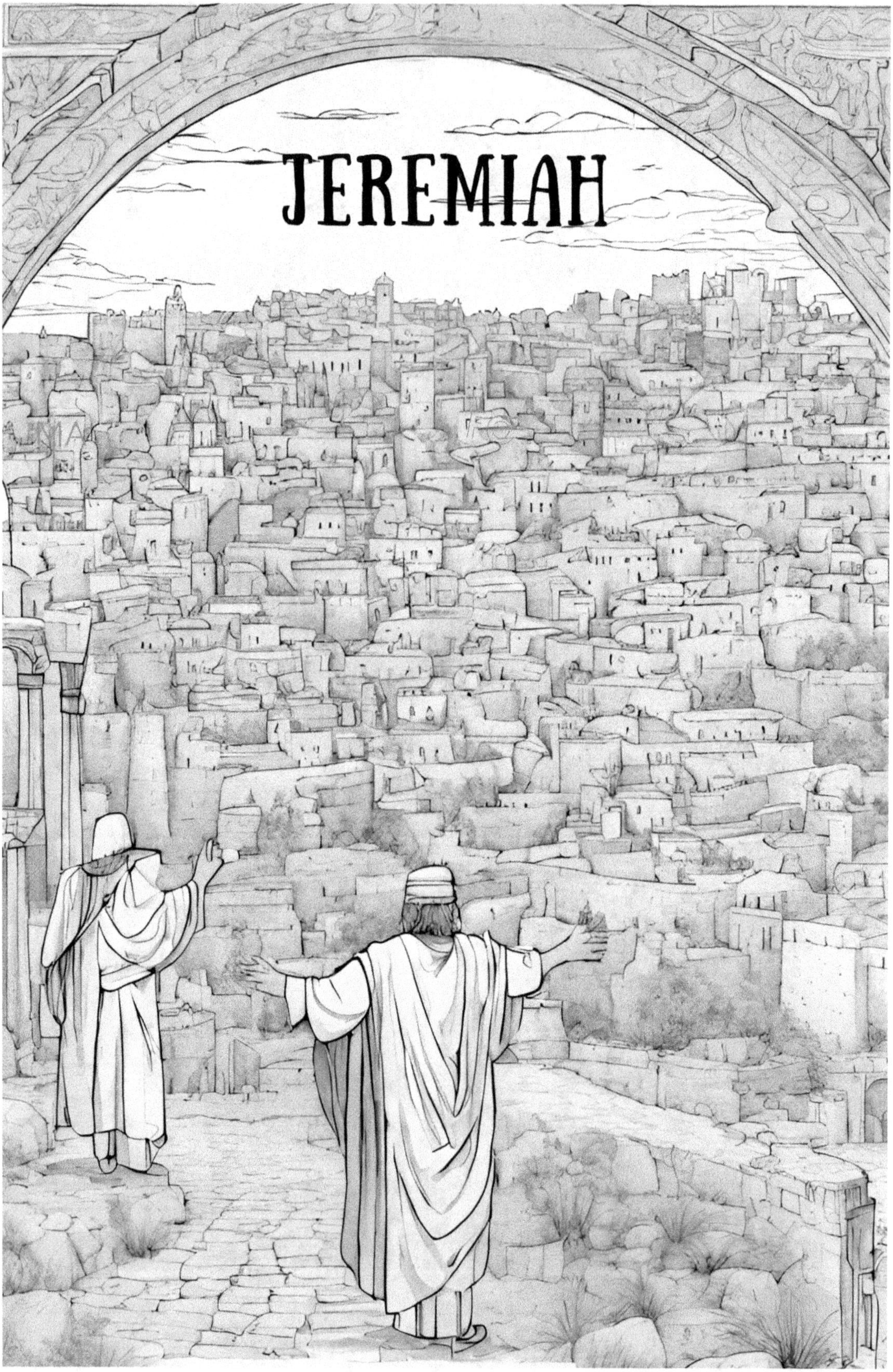
JEREMIAH

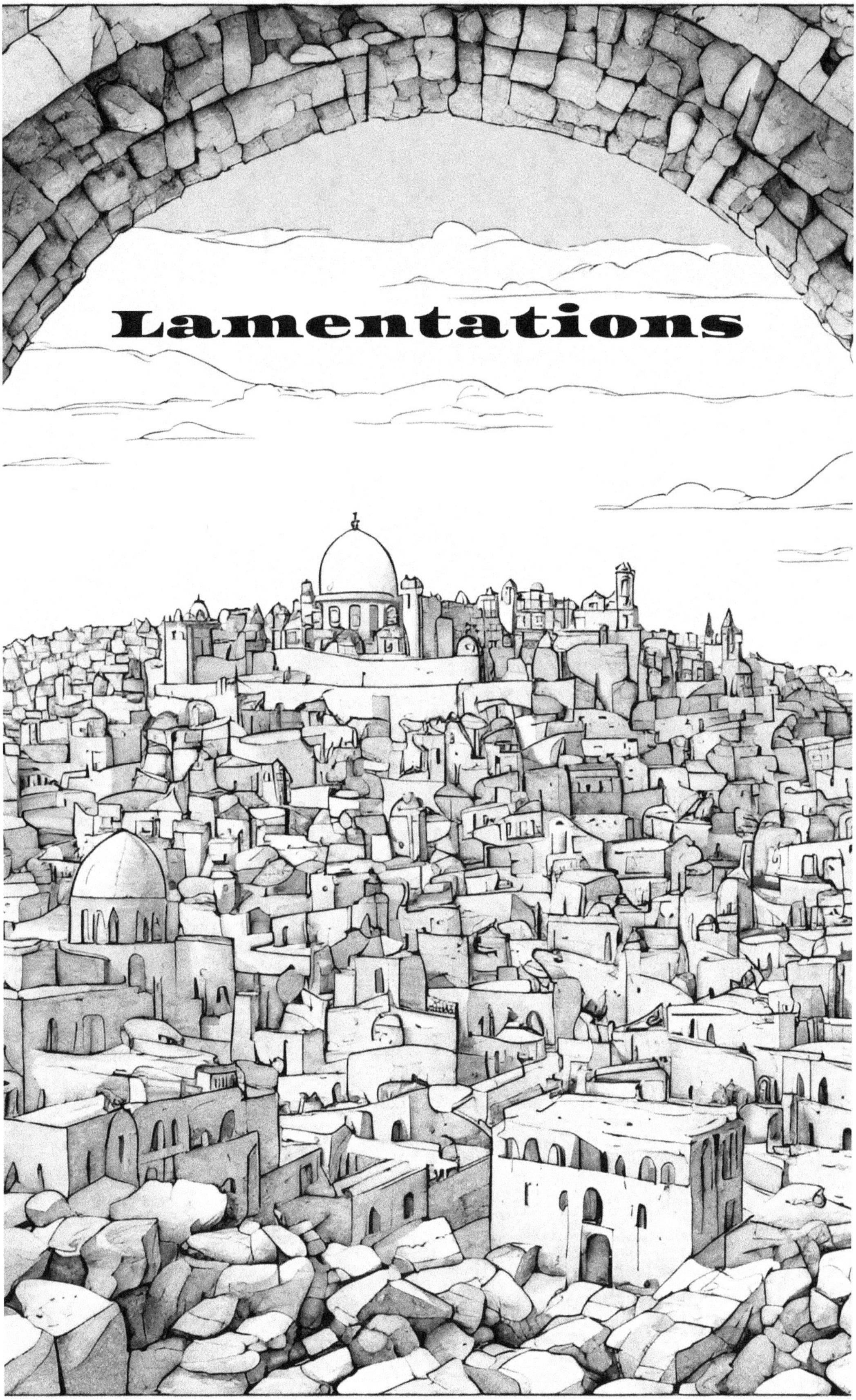
Lamentations

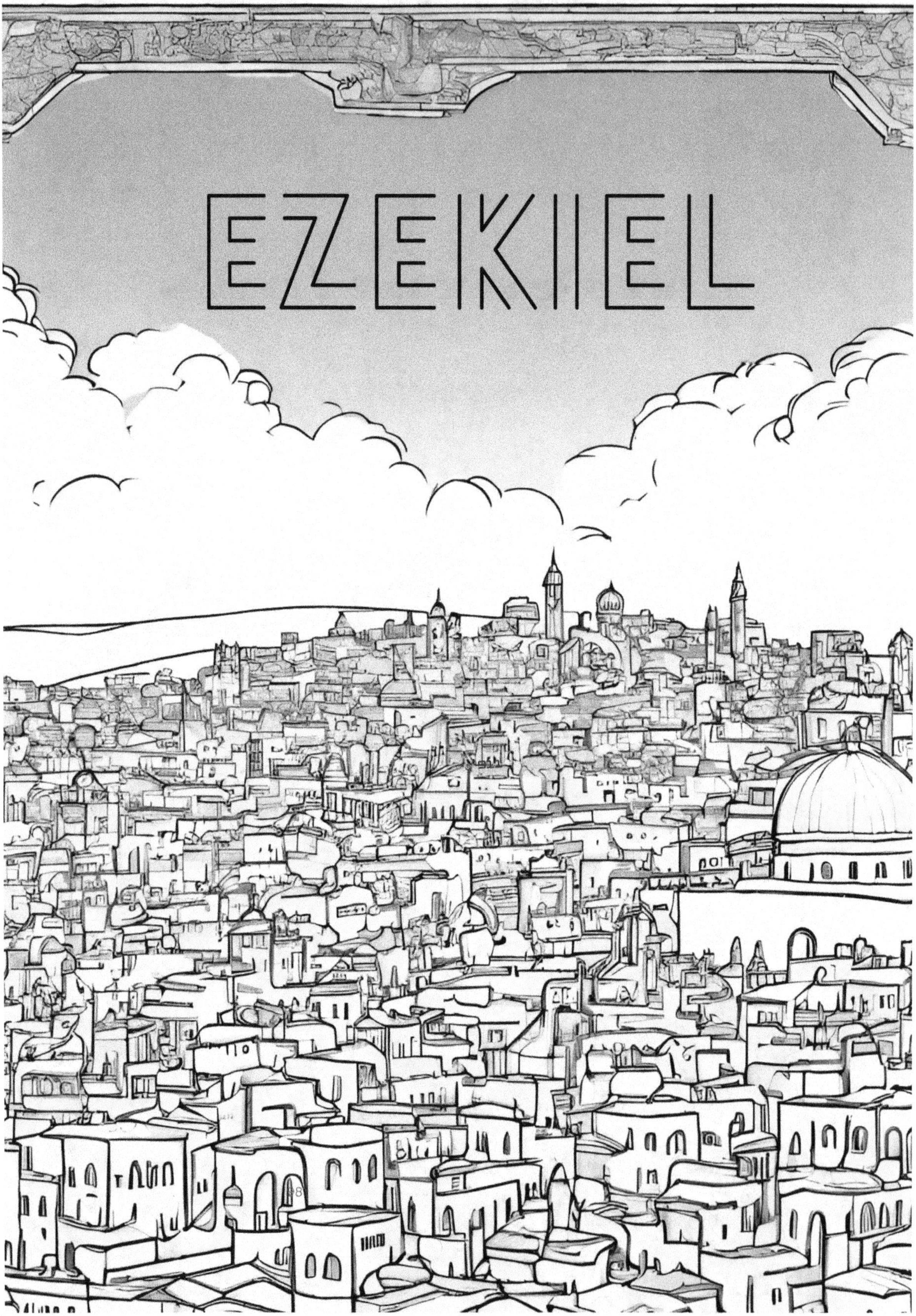
EZEKIEL

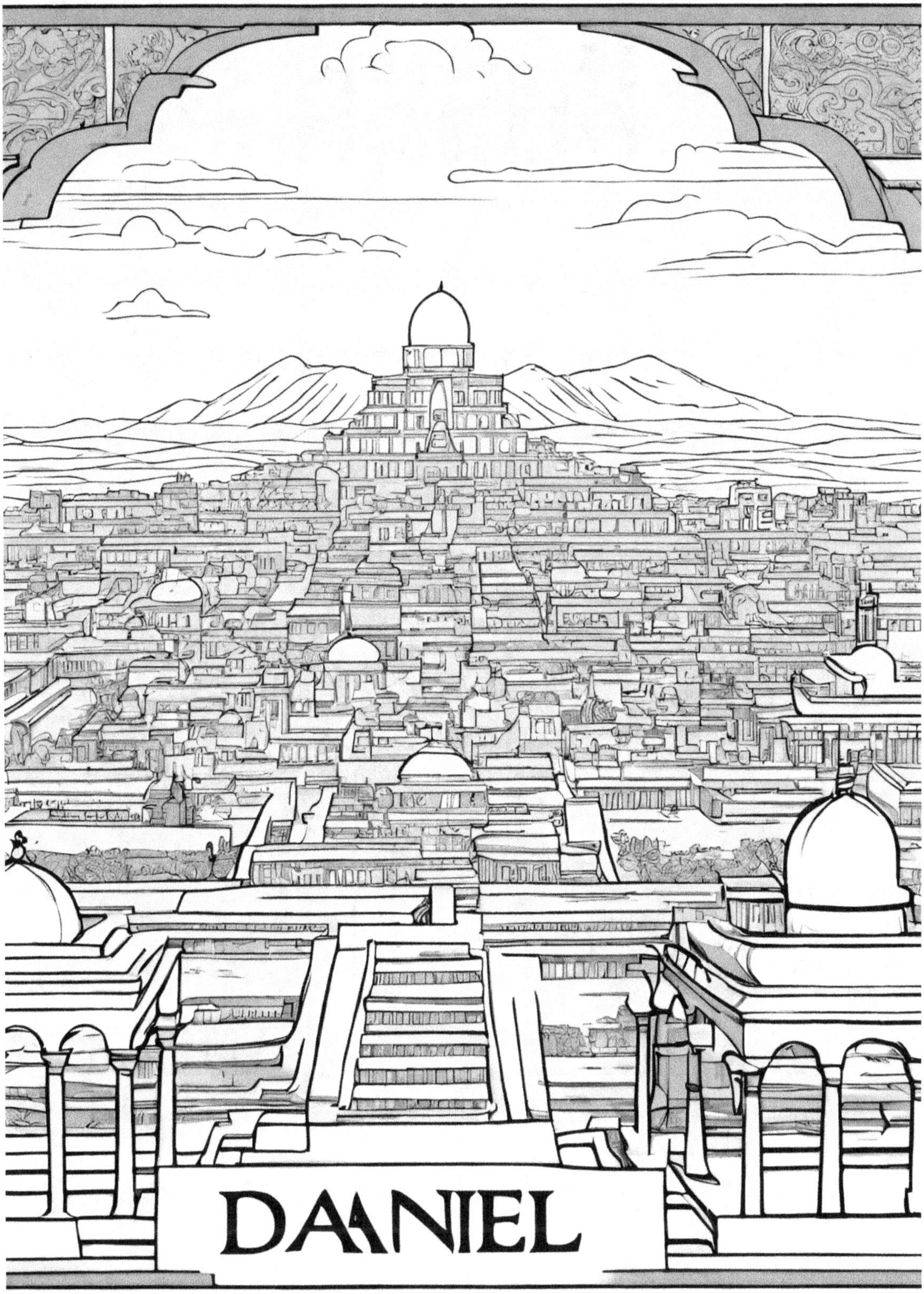
DAANIEL

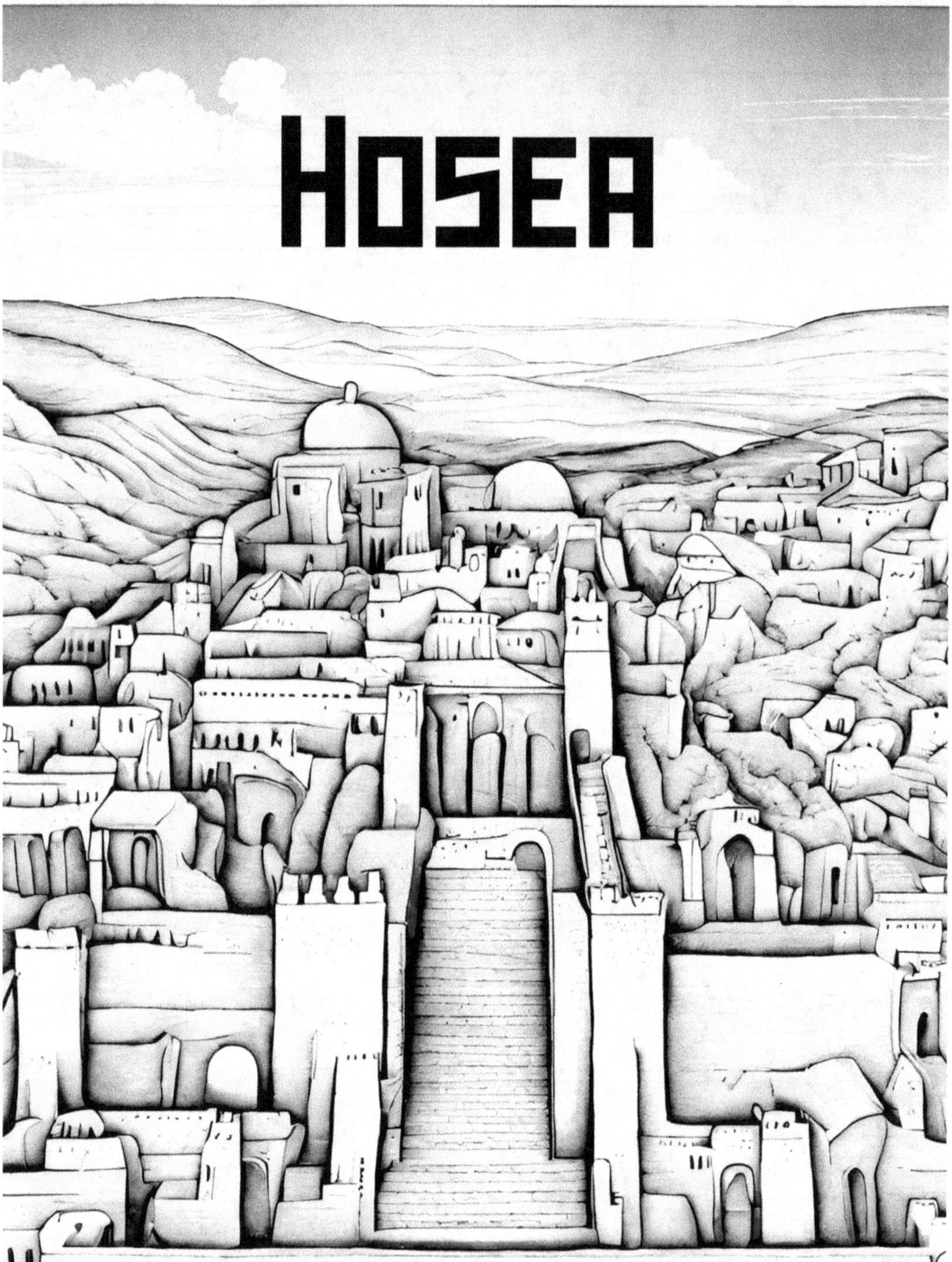
HOSEA

JOEL

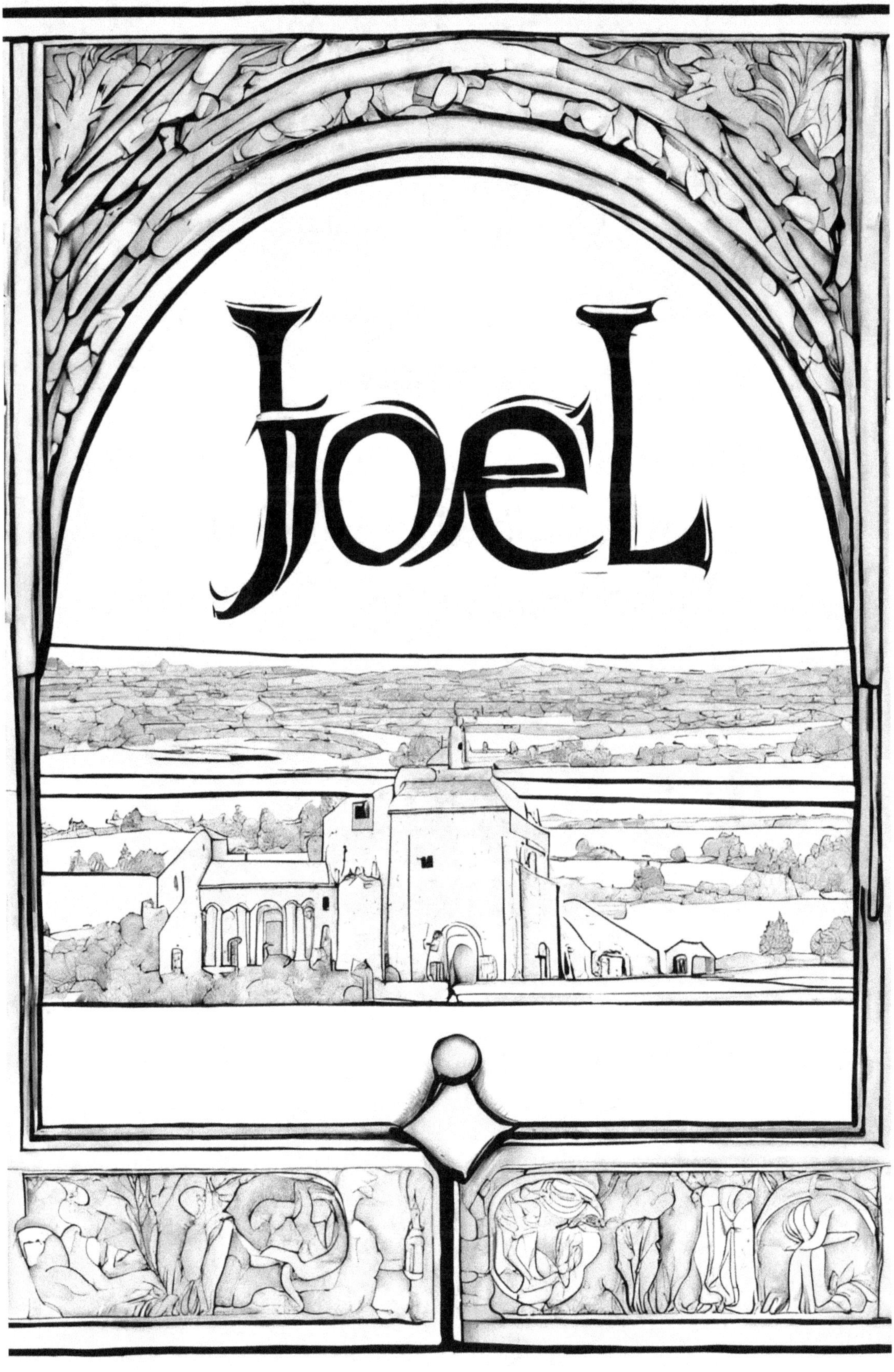

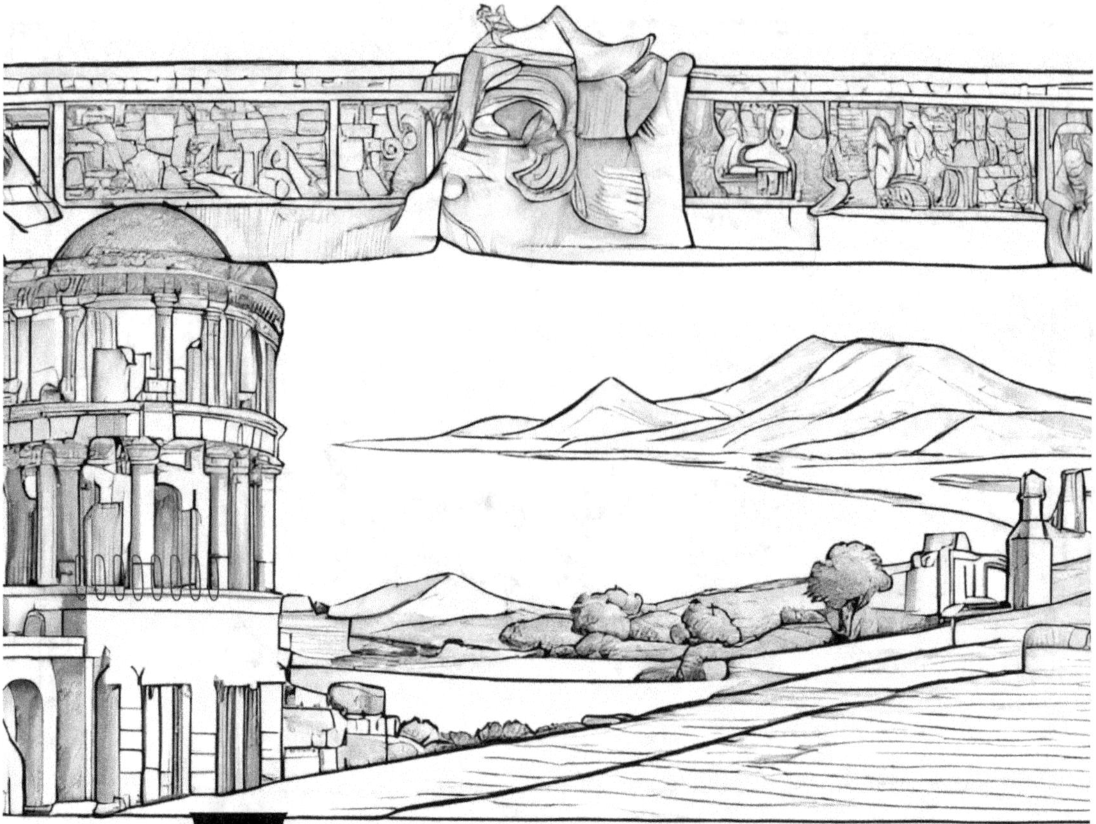

Amos

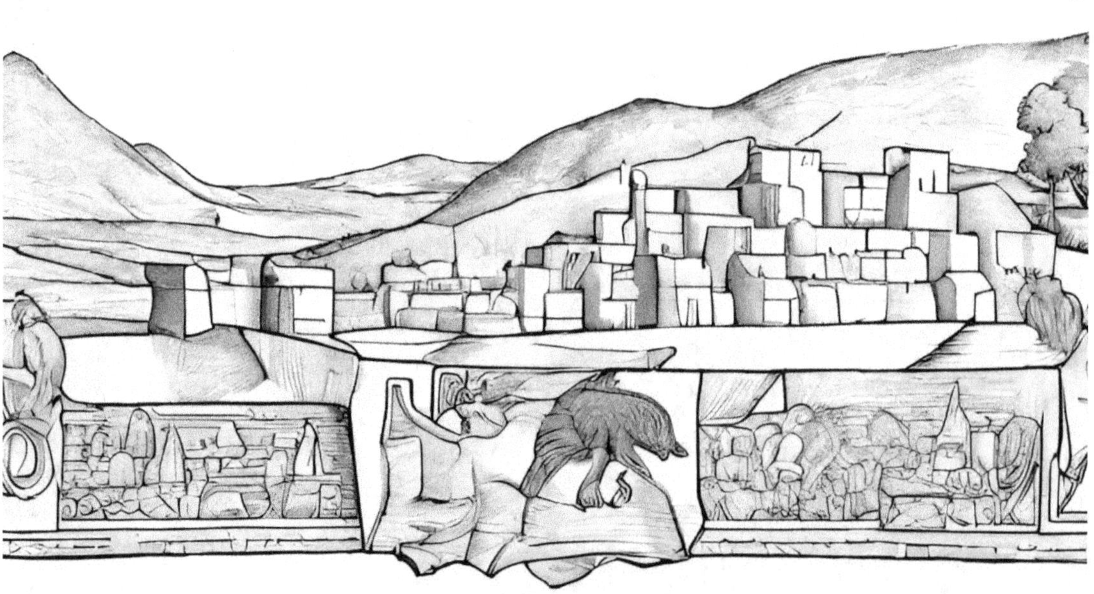

OBADIAH

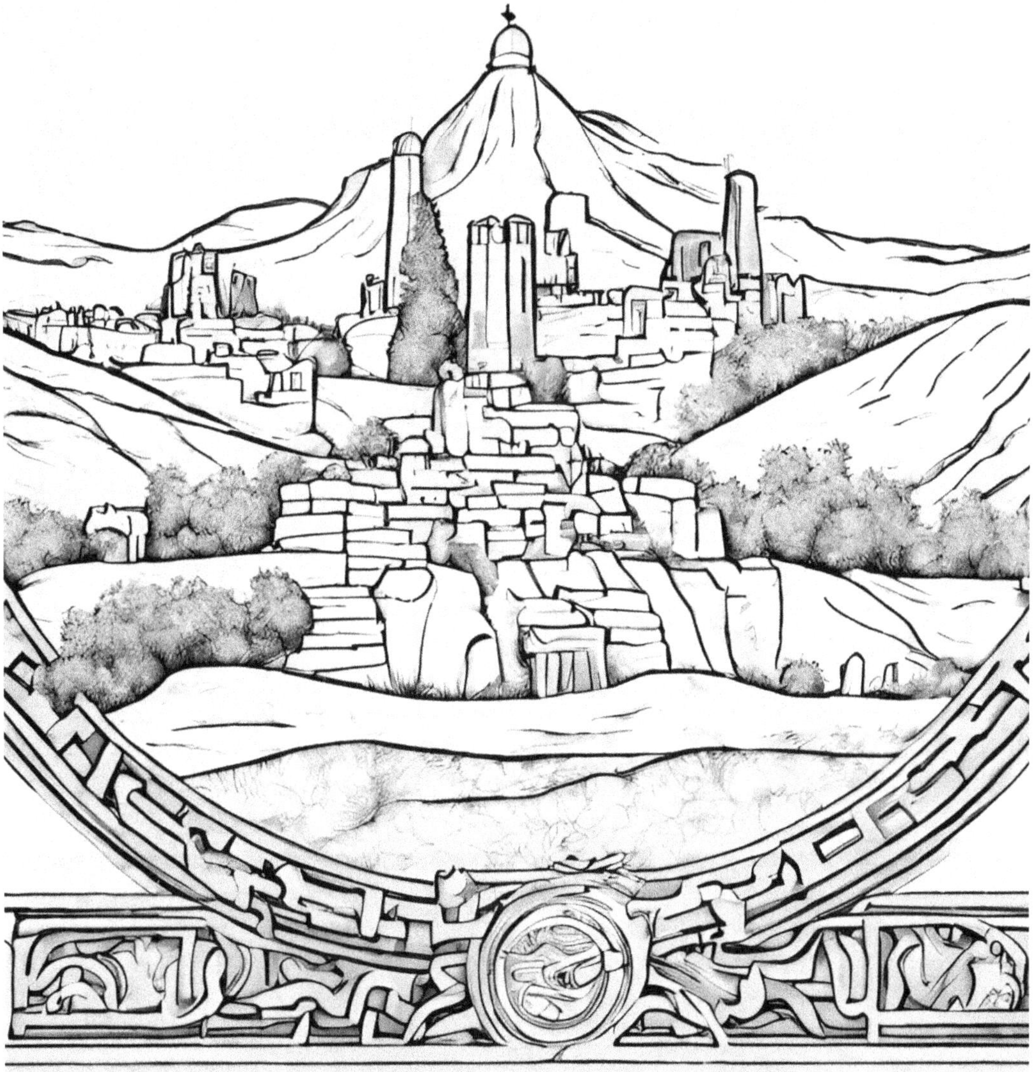

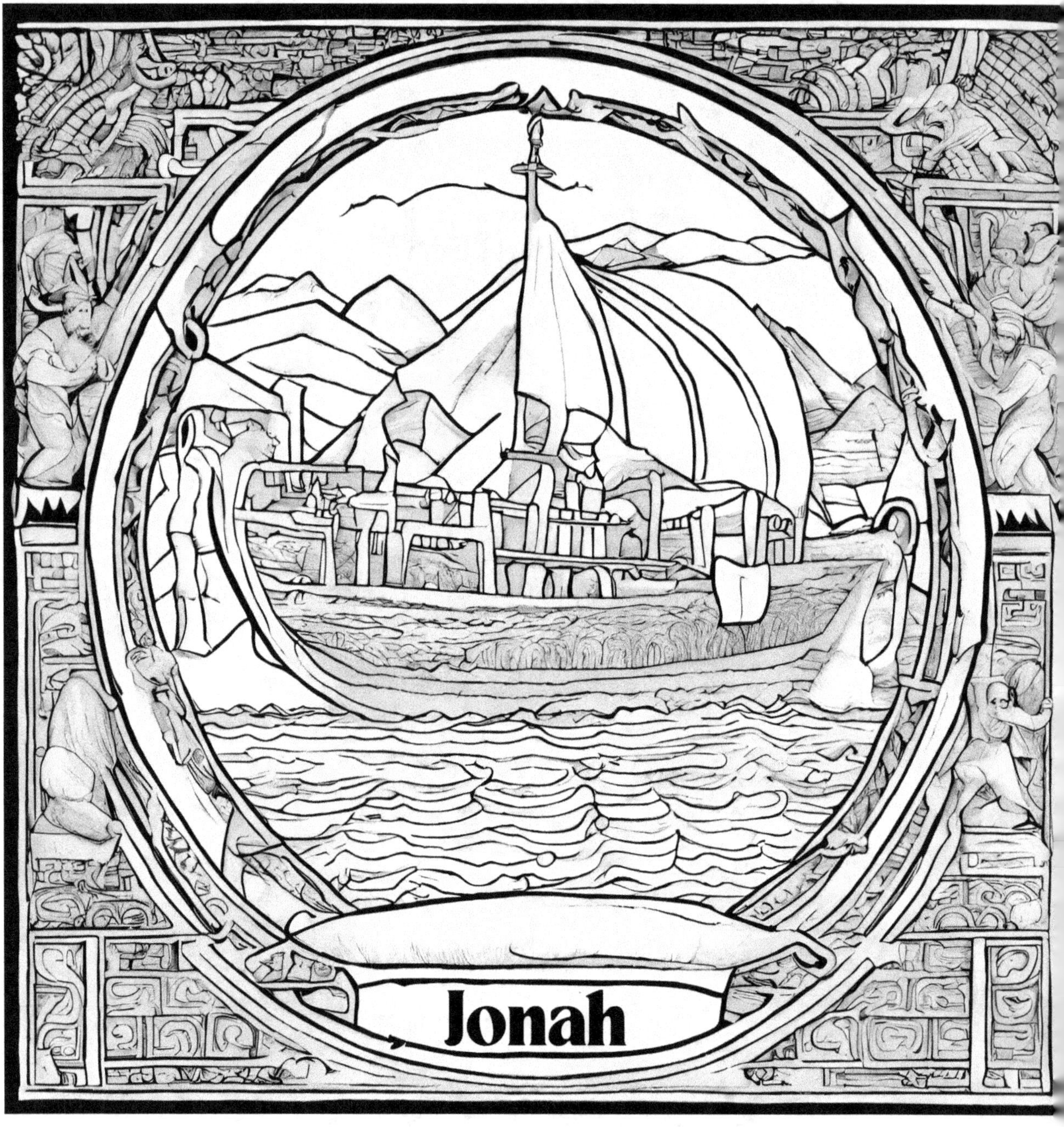
Jonah

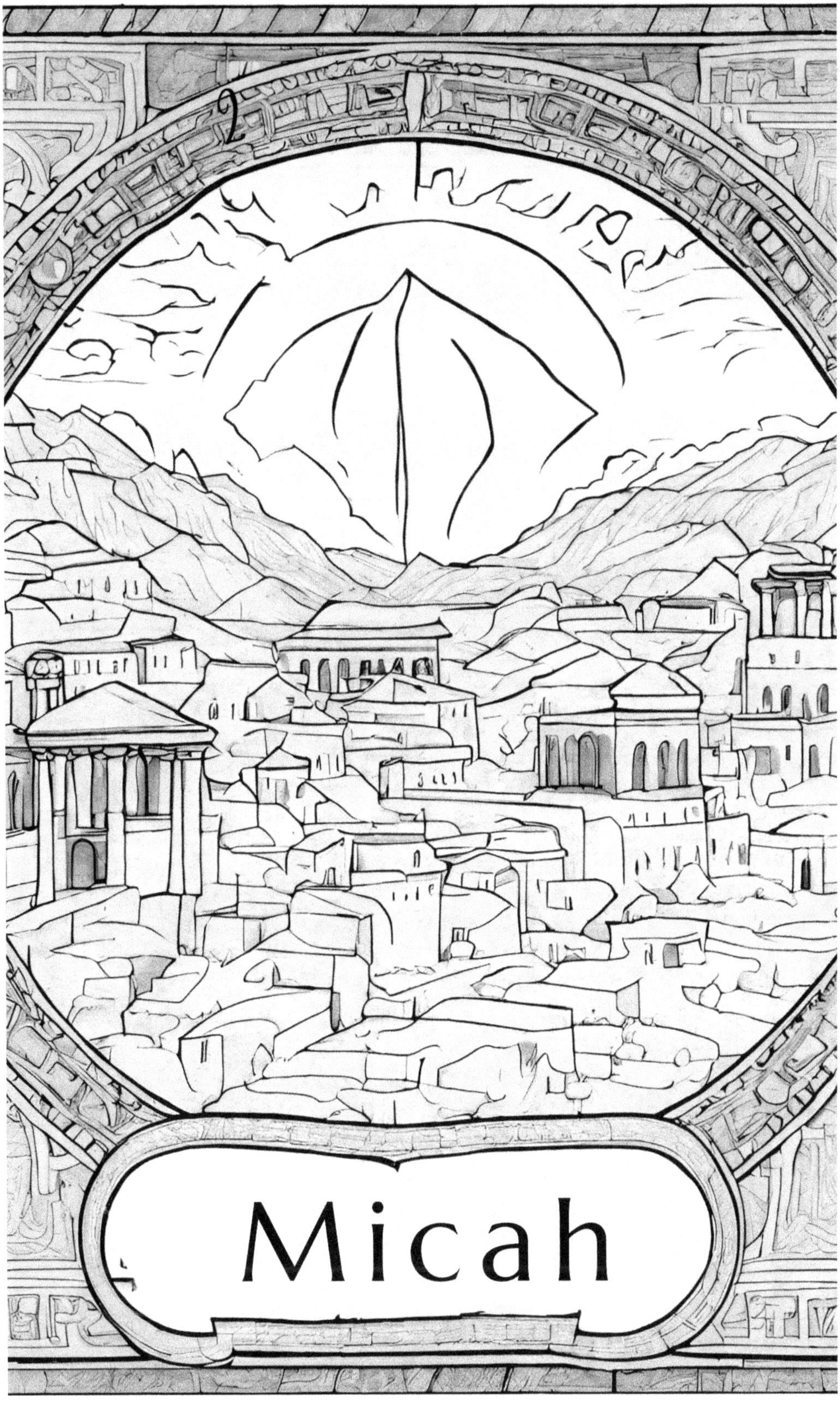
Micah

NAHUM

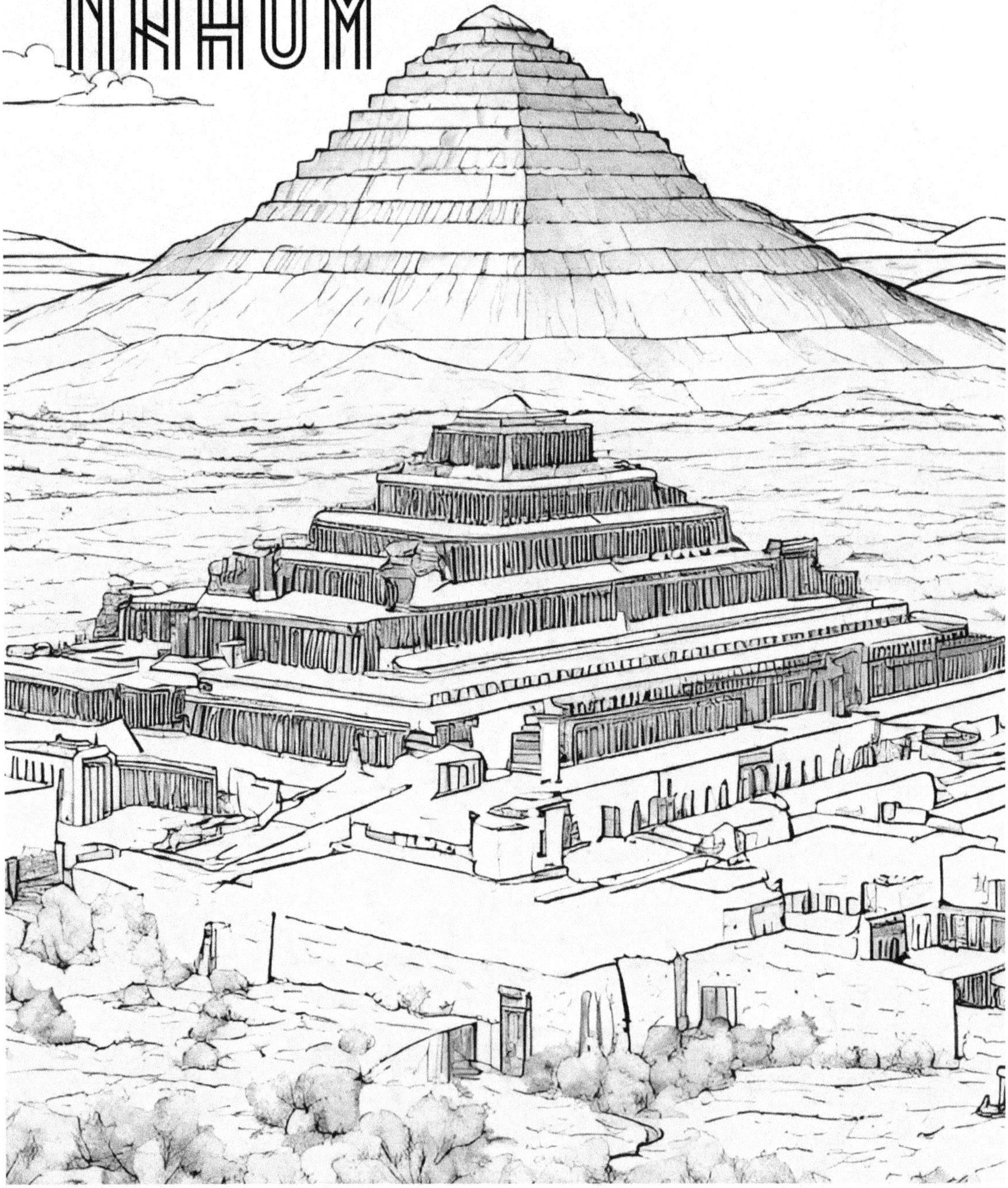

Habakkuk

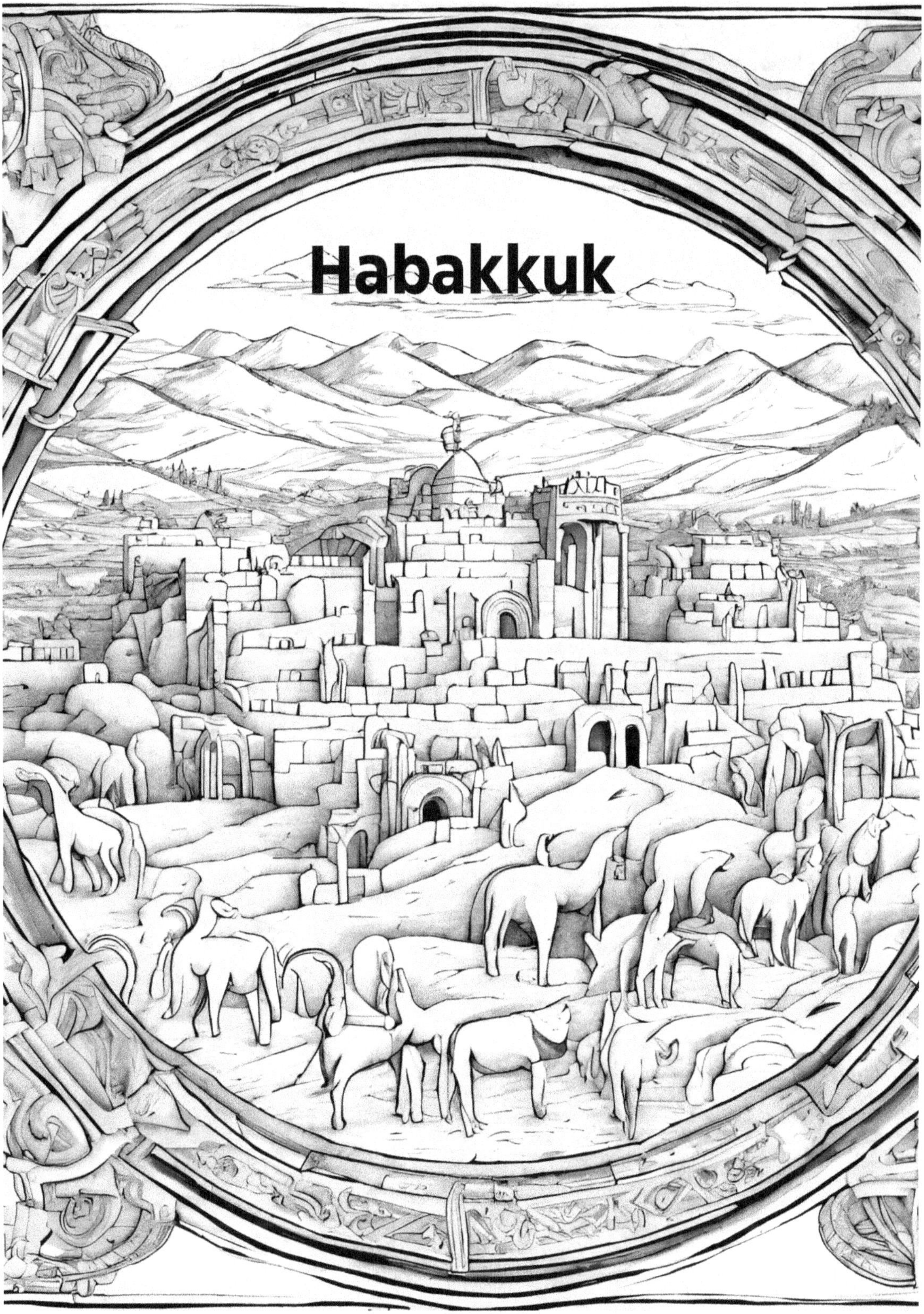

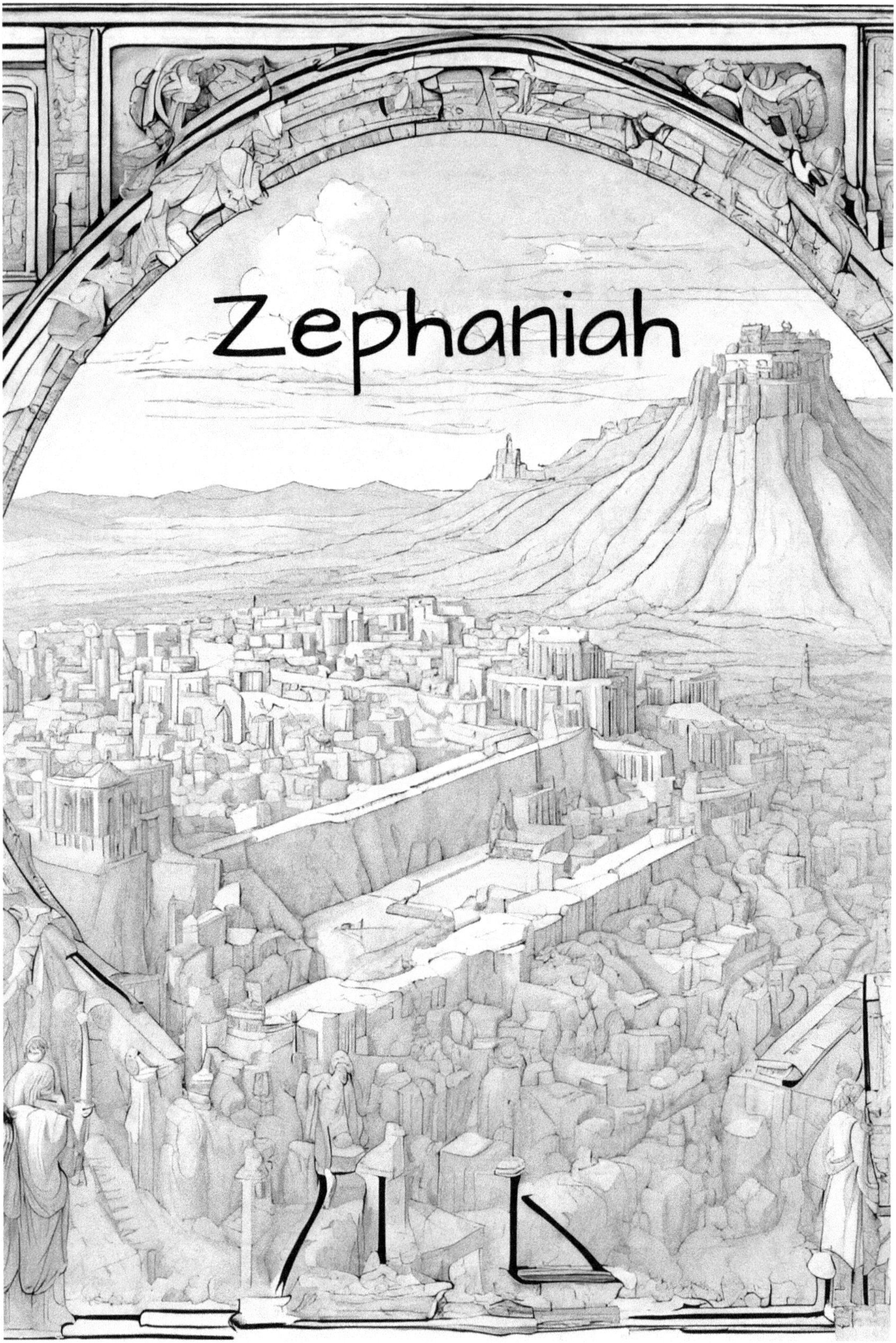
Zephaniah

HAGGAI

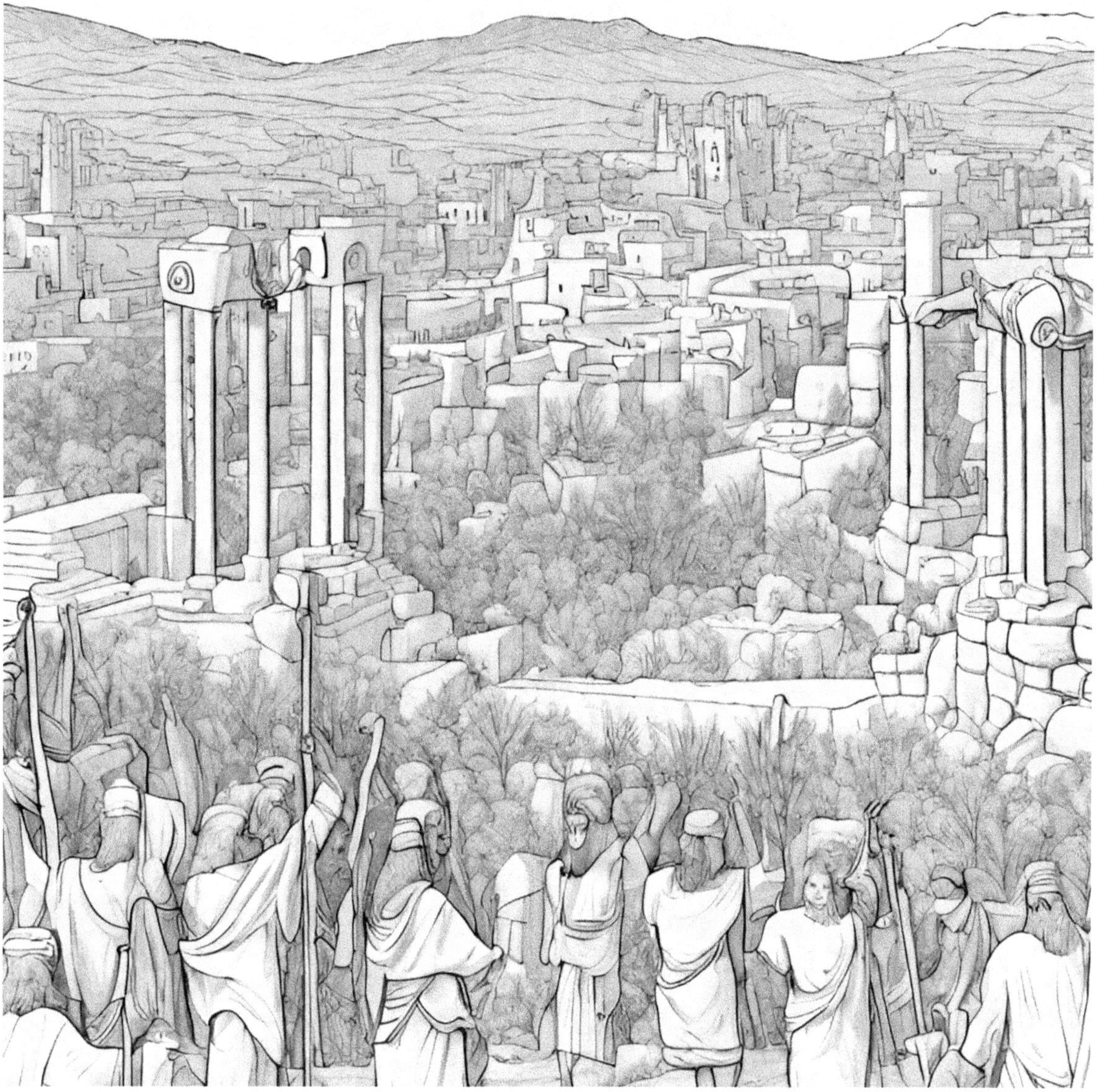

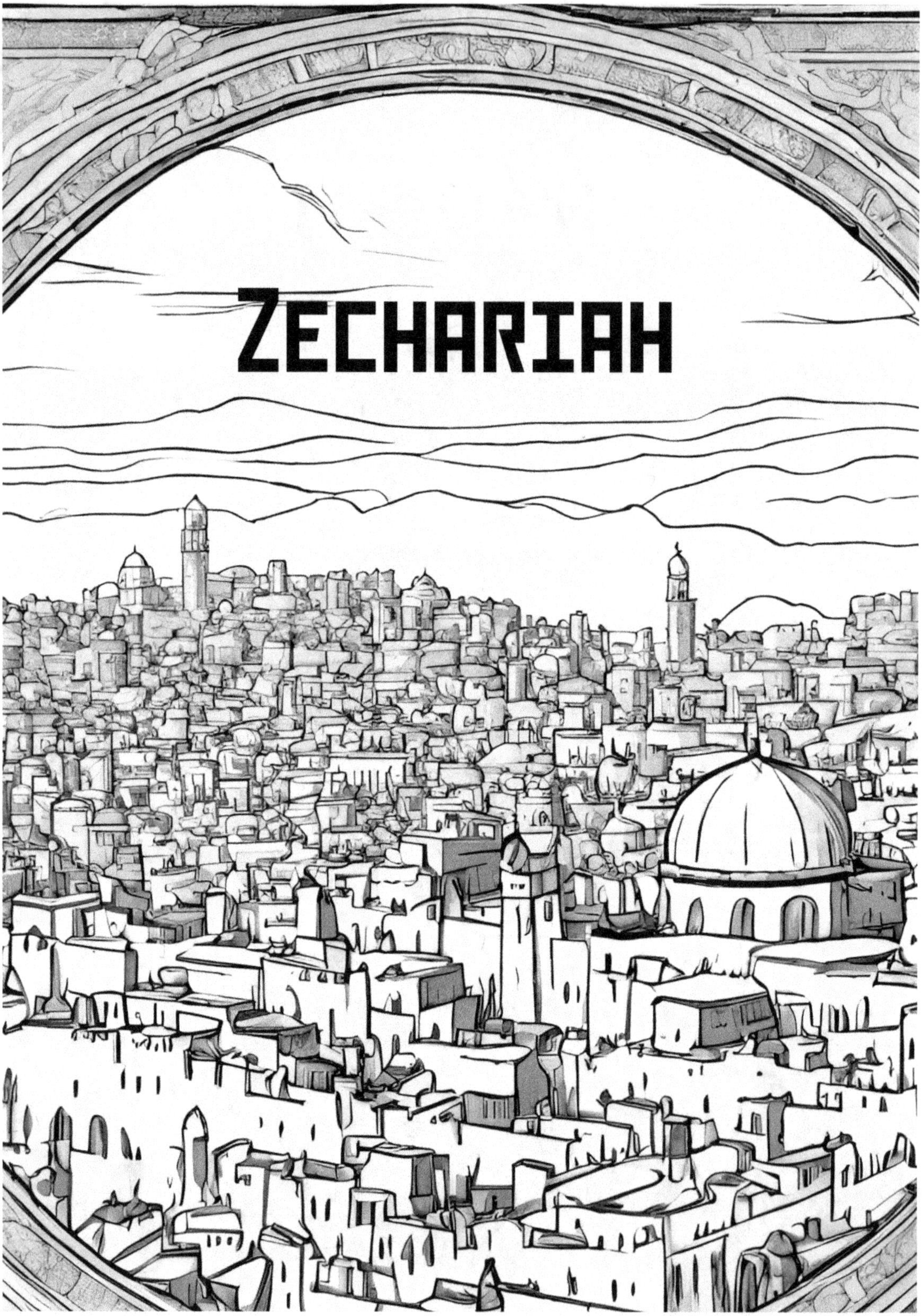
ZECHARIAH

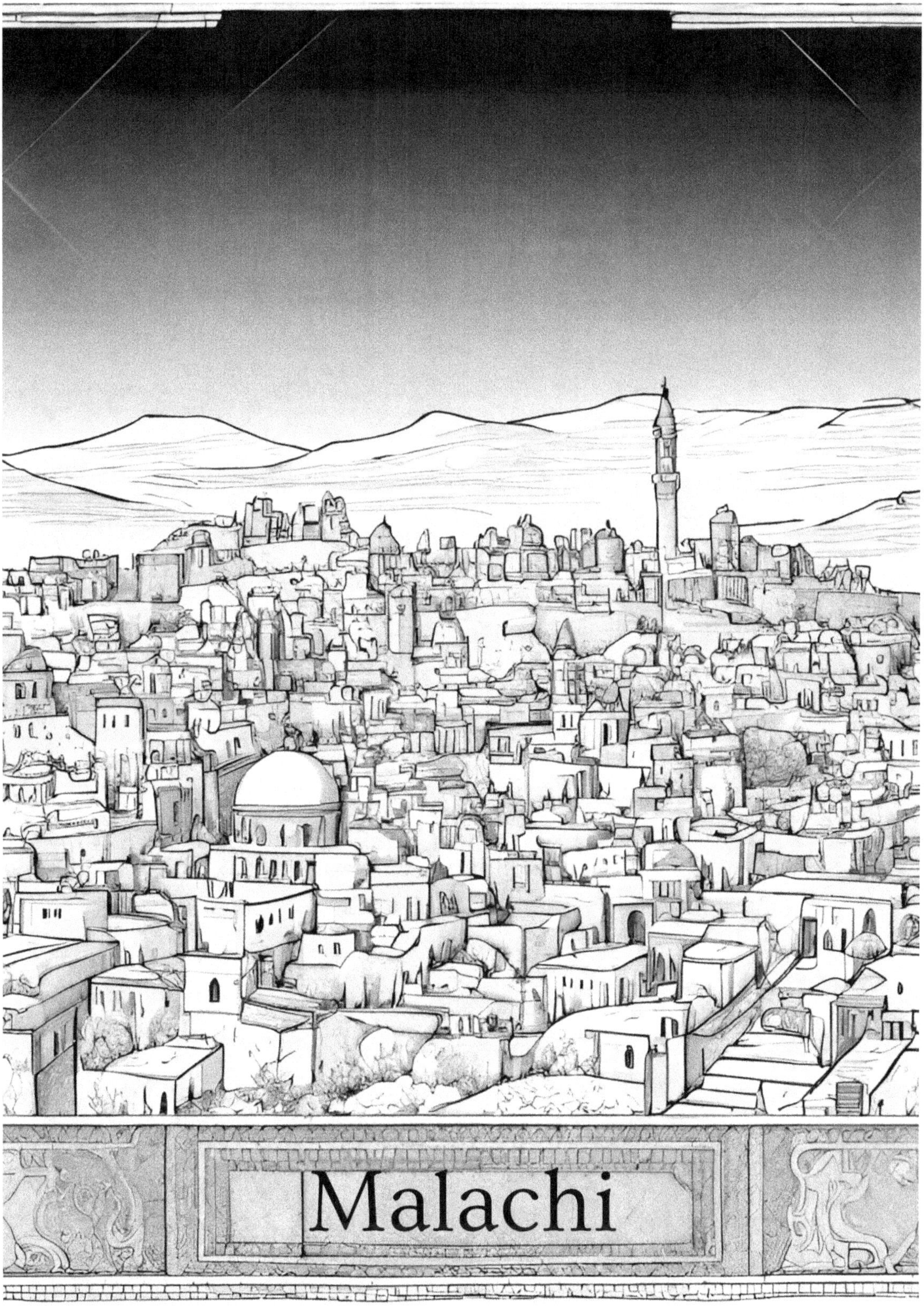

Malachi

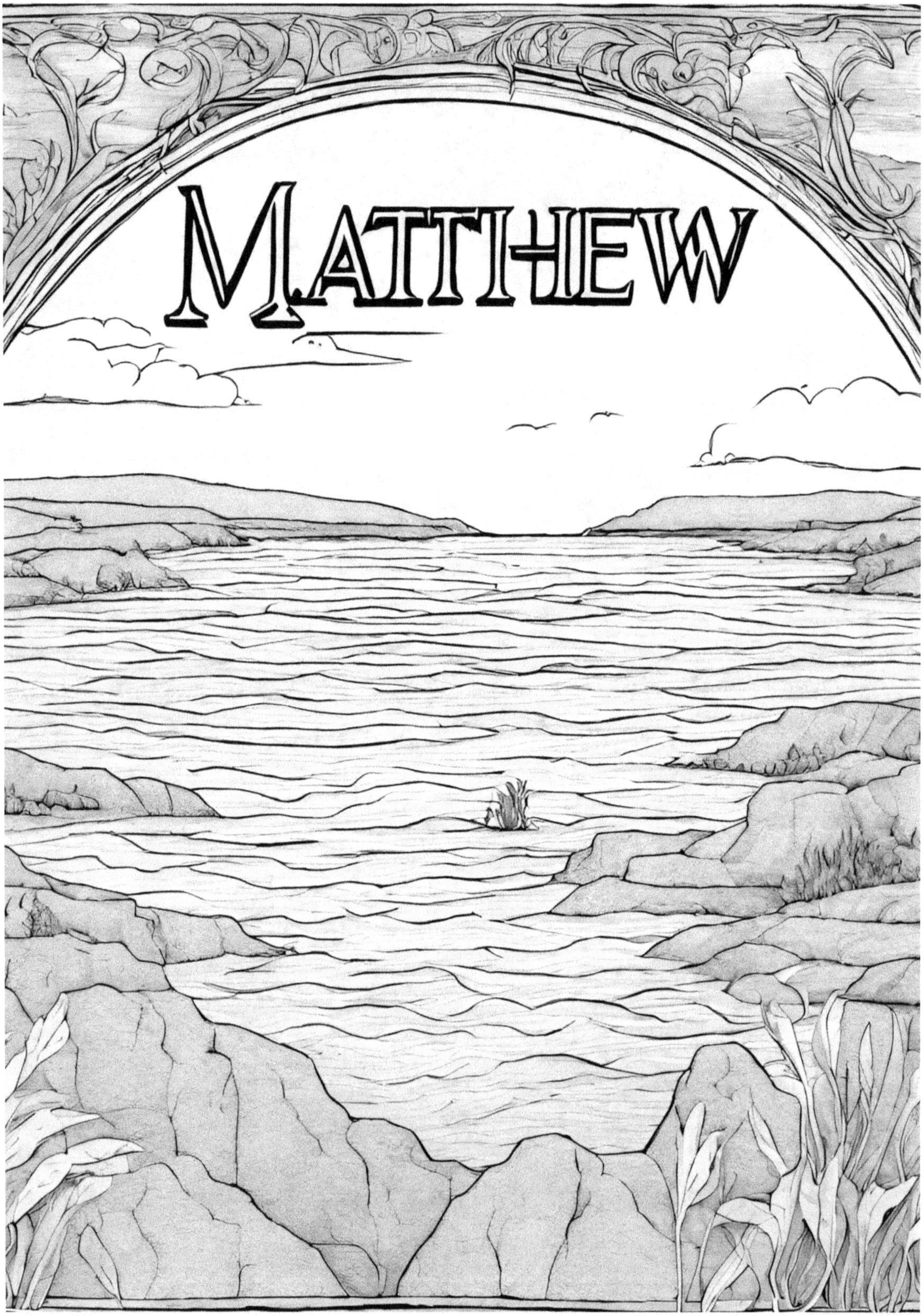
MATTHEW

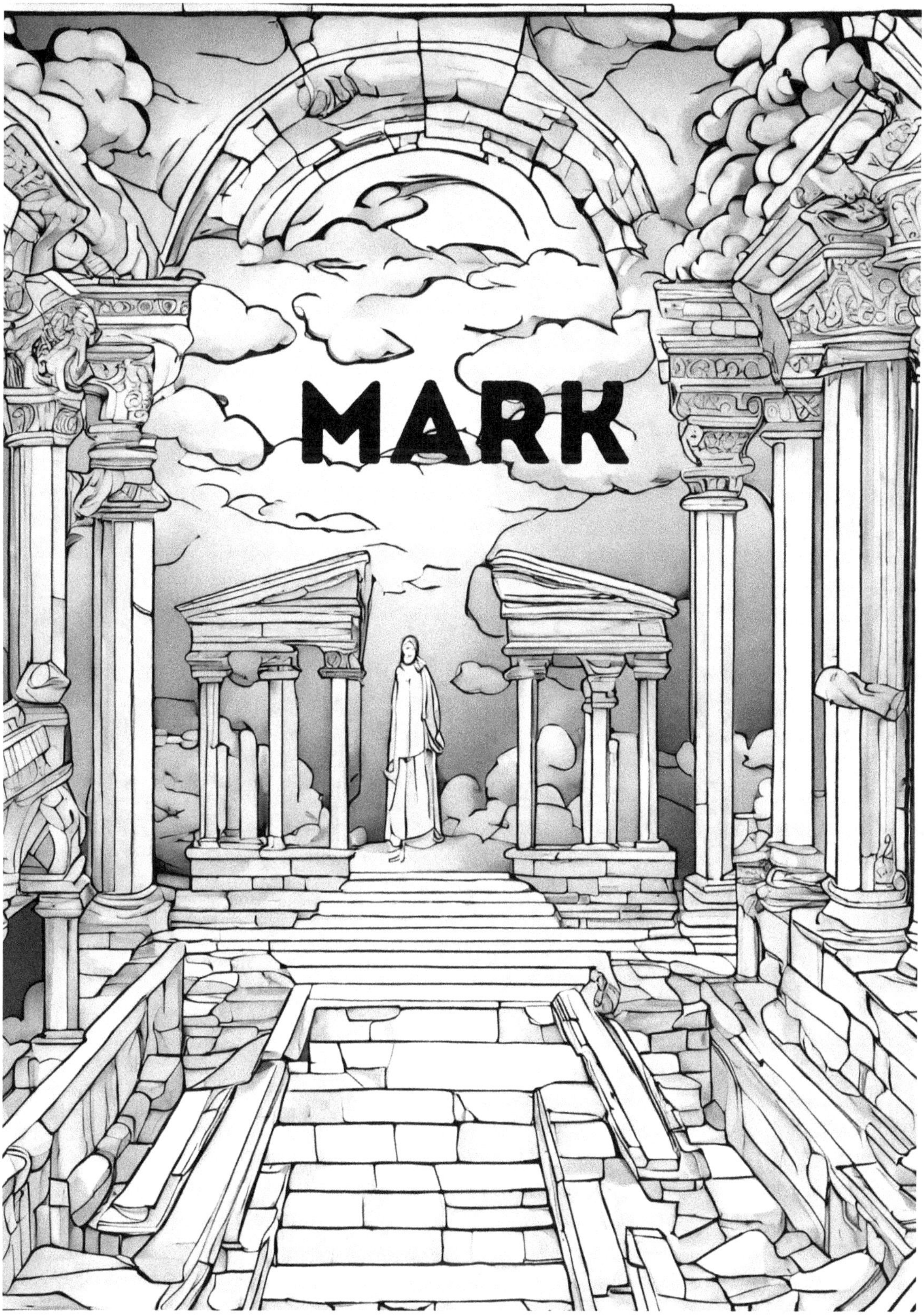
MARK

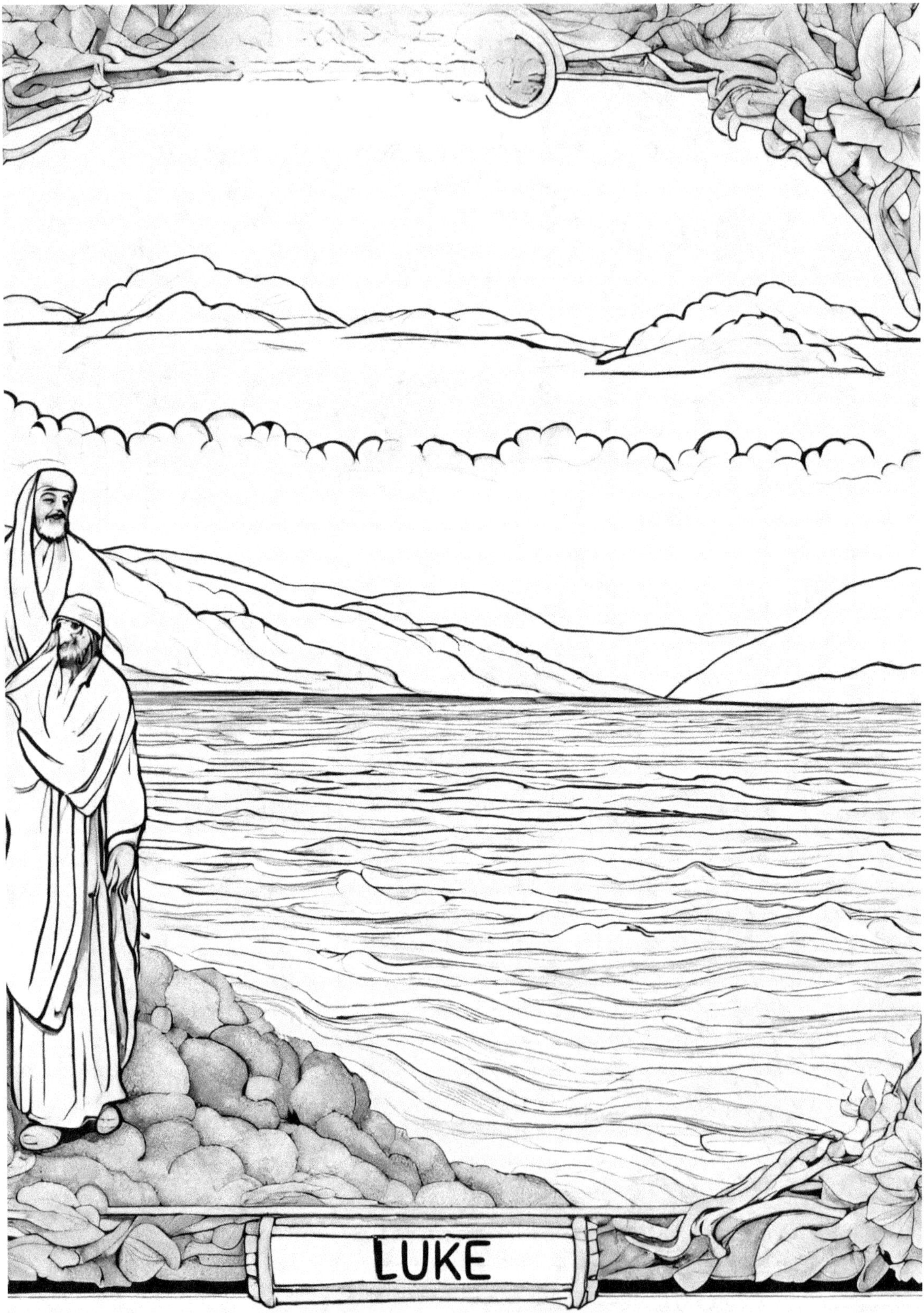
LUKE

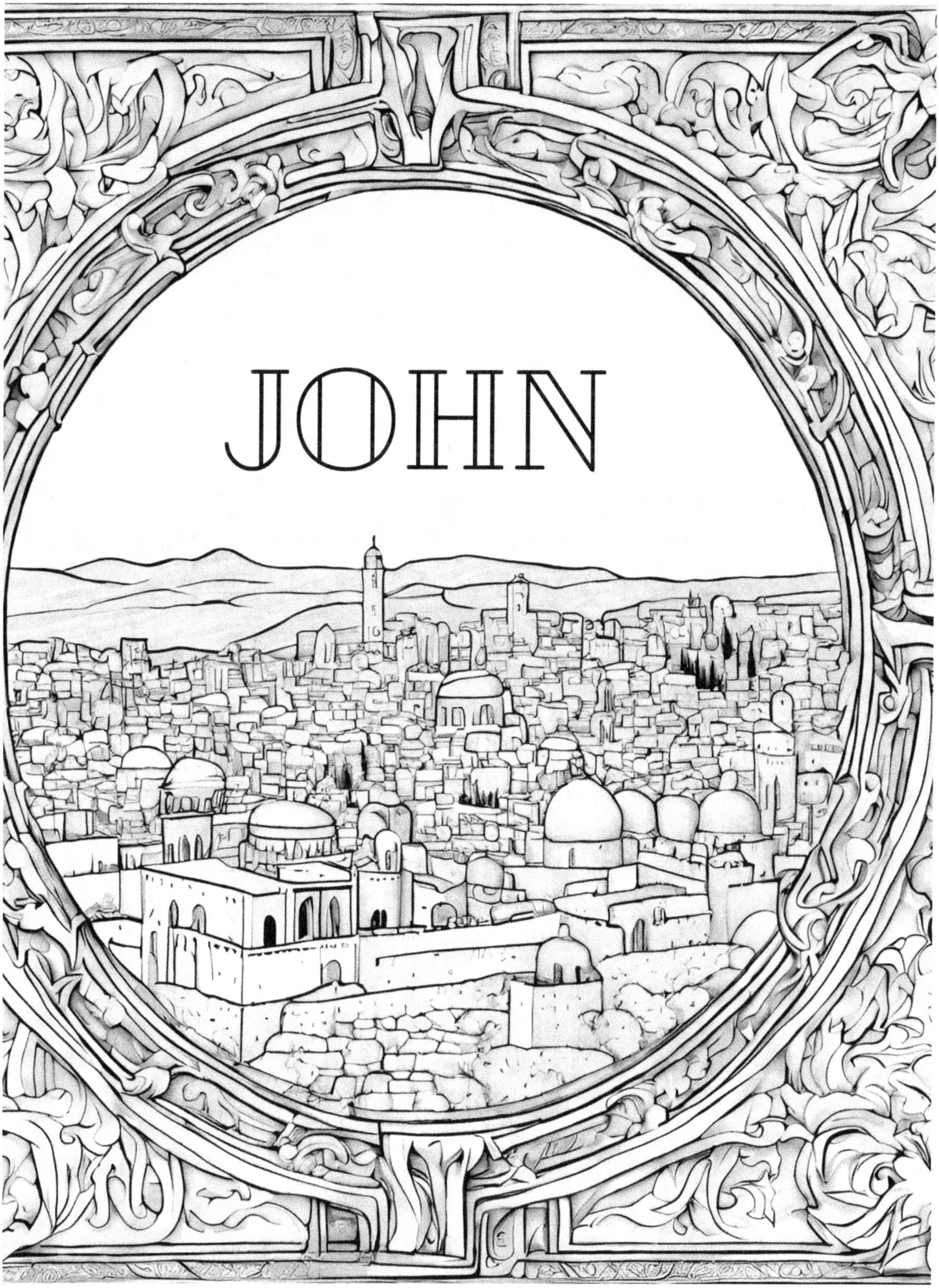
JOHN

ACTS

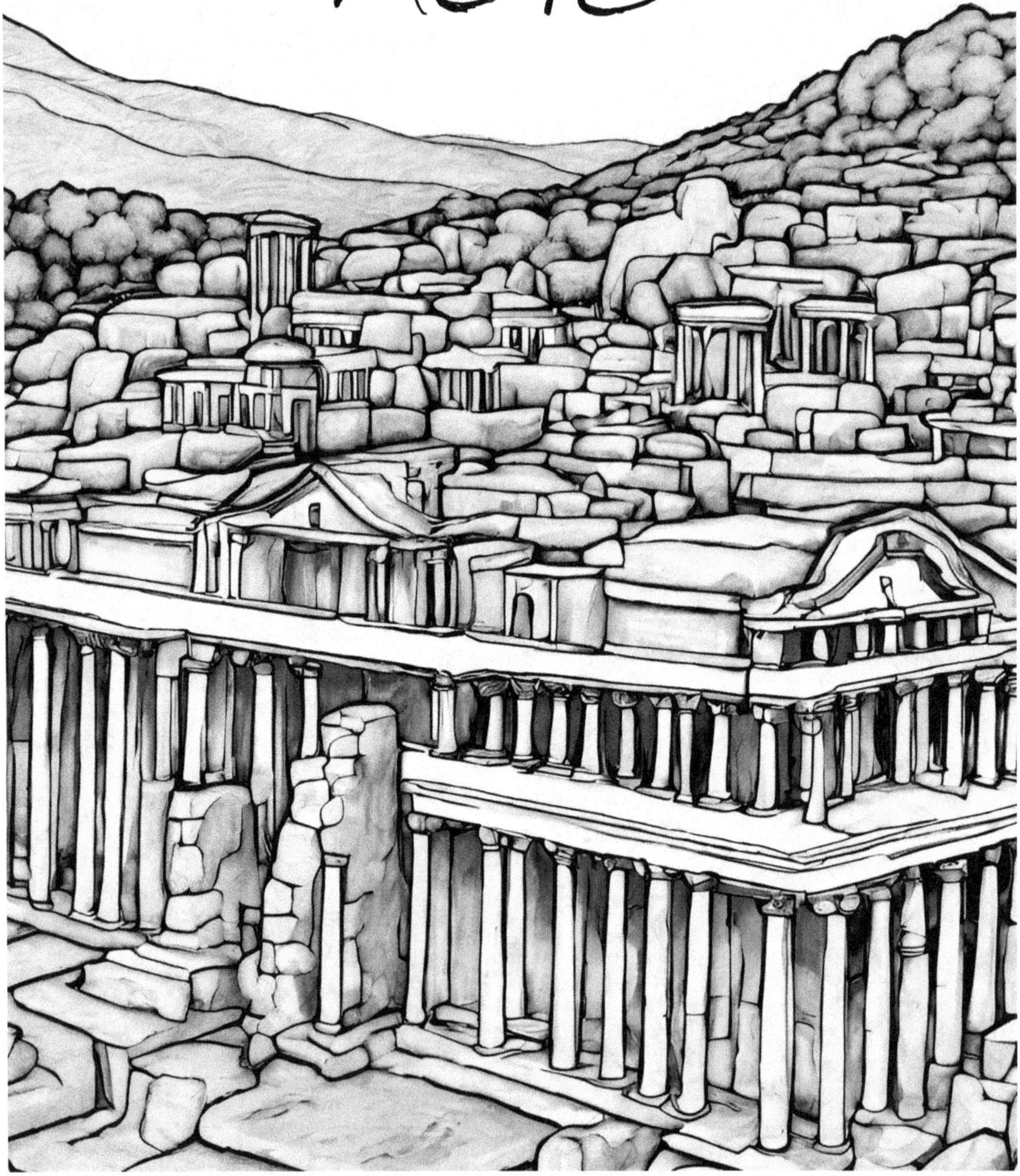

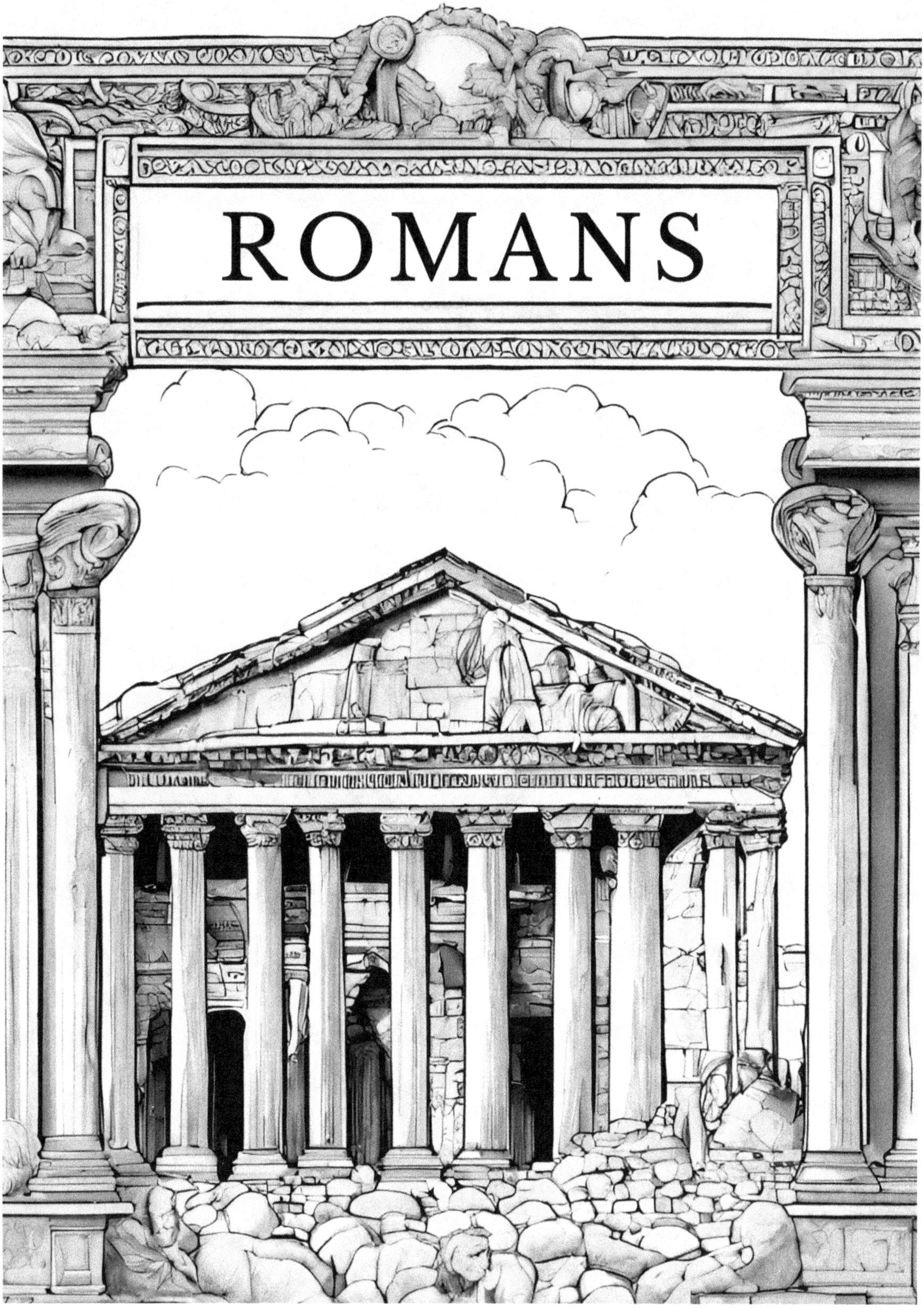
ROMANS

1 & 2 Corinthians

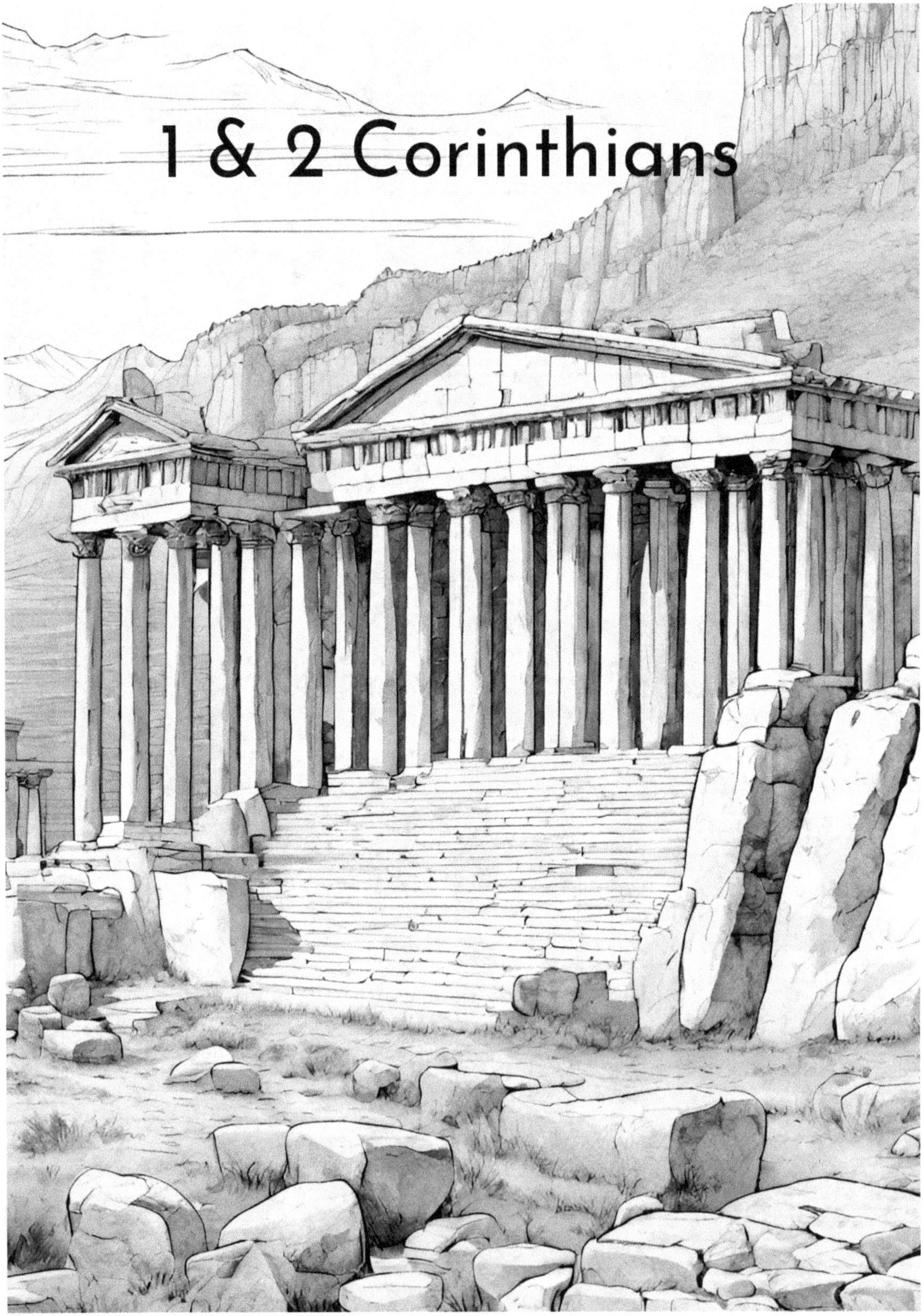

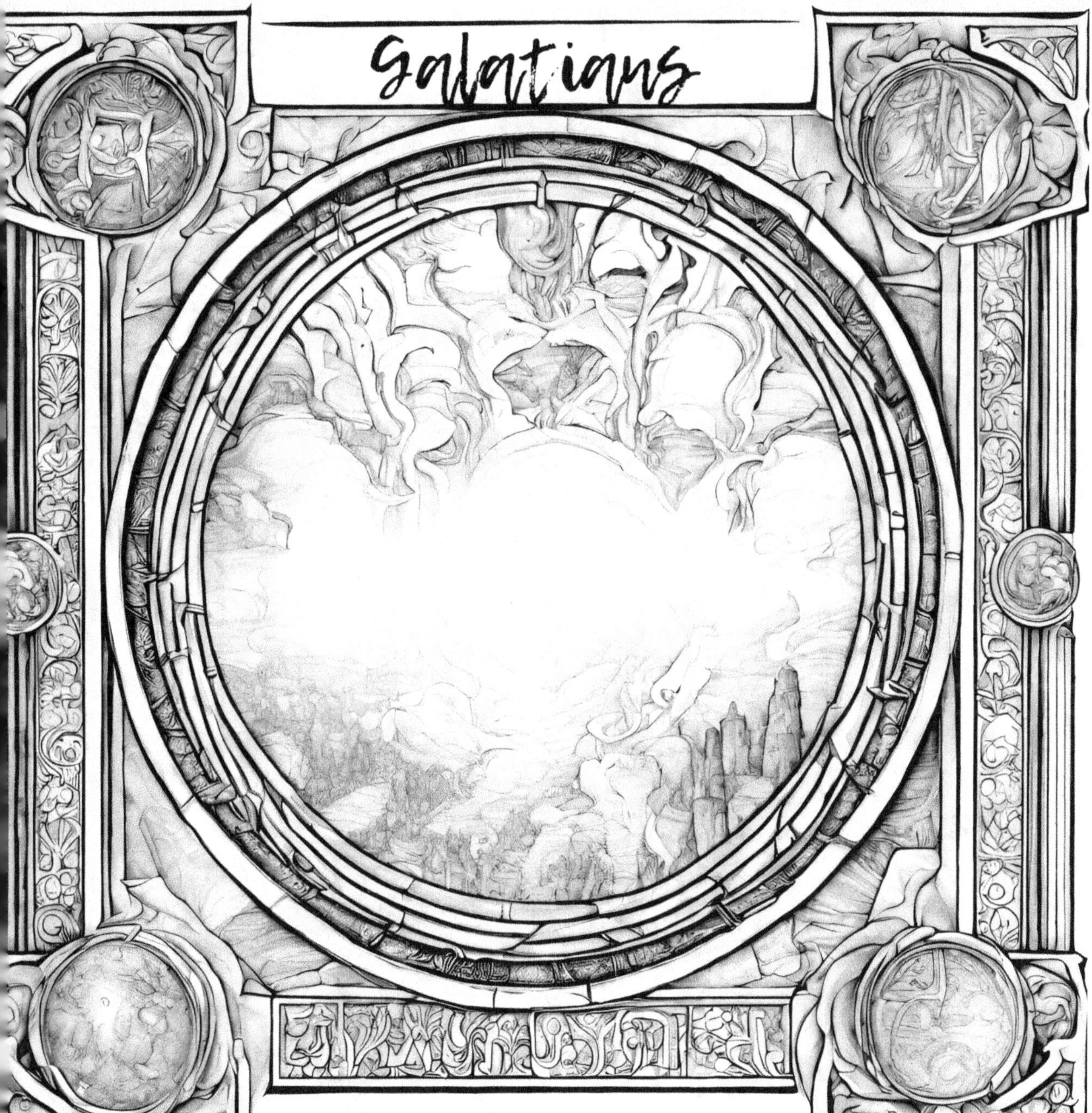
Galatians

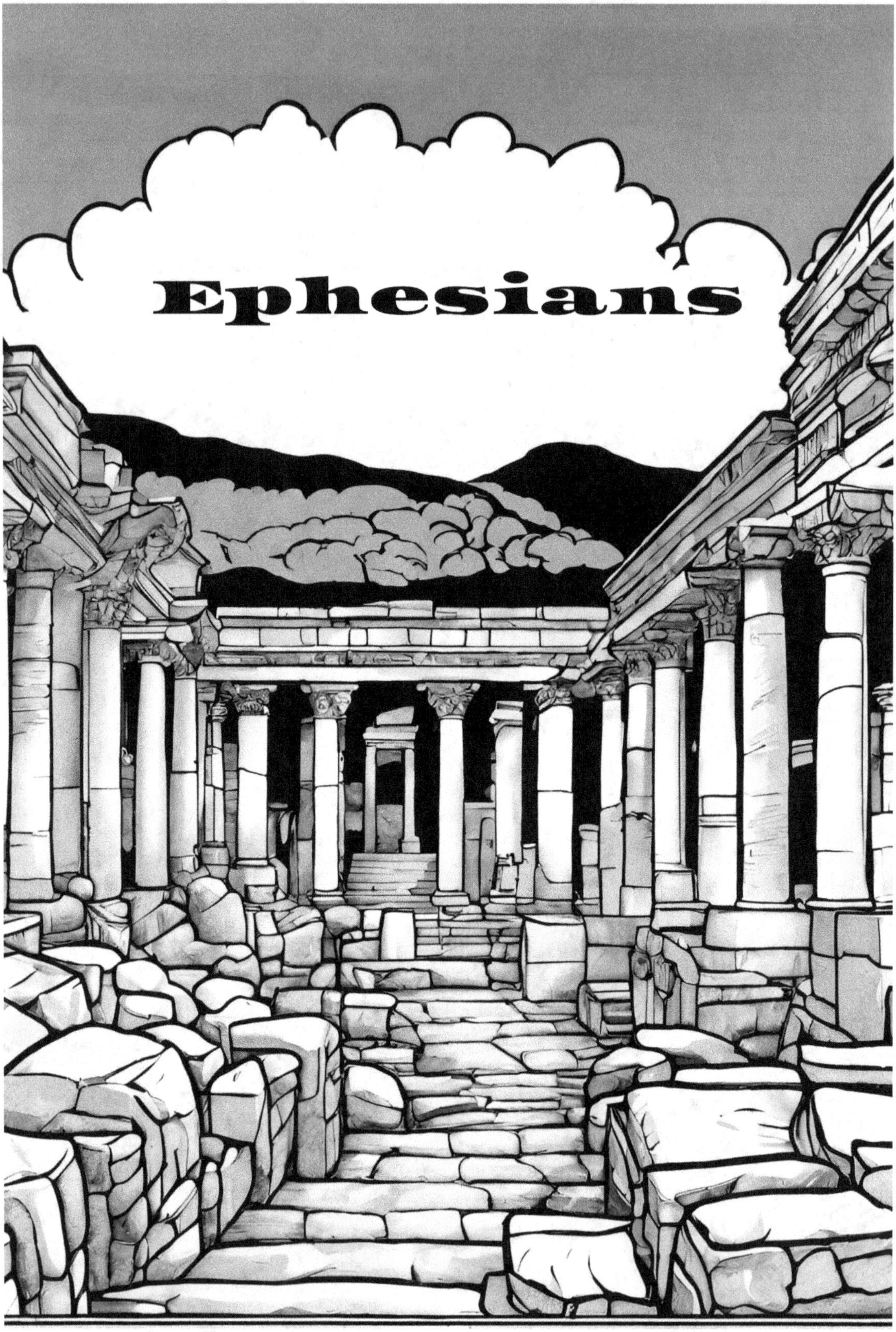
Ephesians

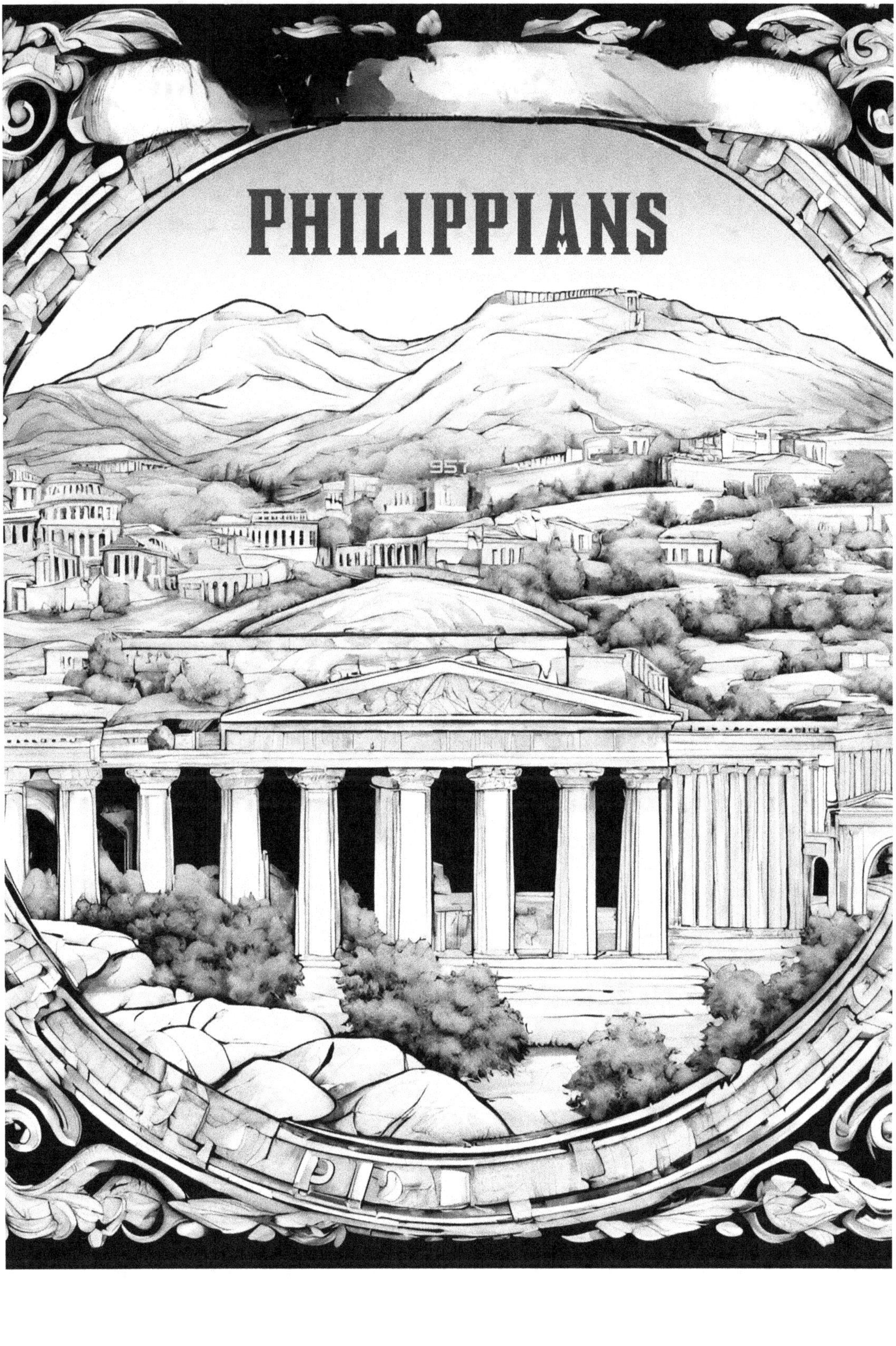
PHILIPPIANS

1 & 2 Thessalonians

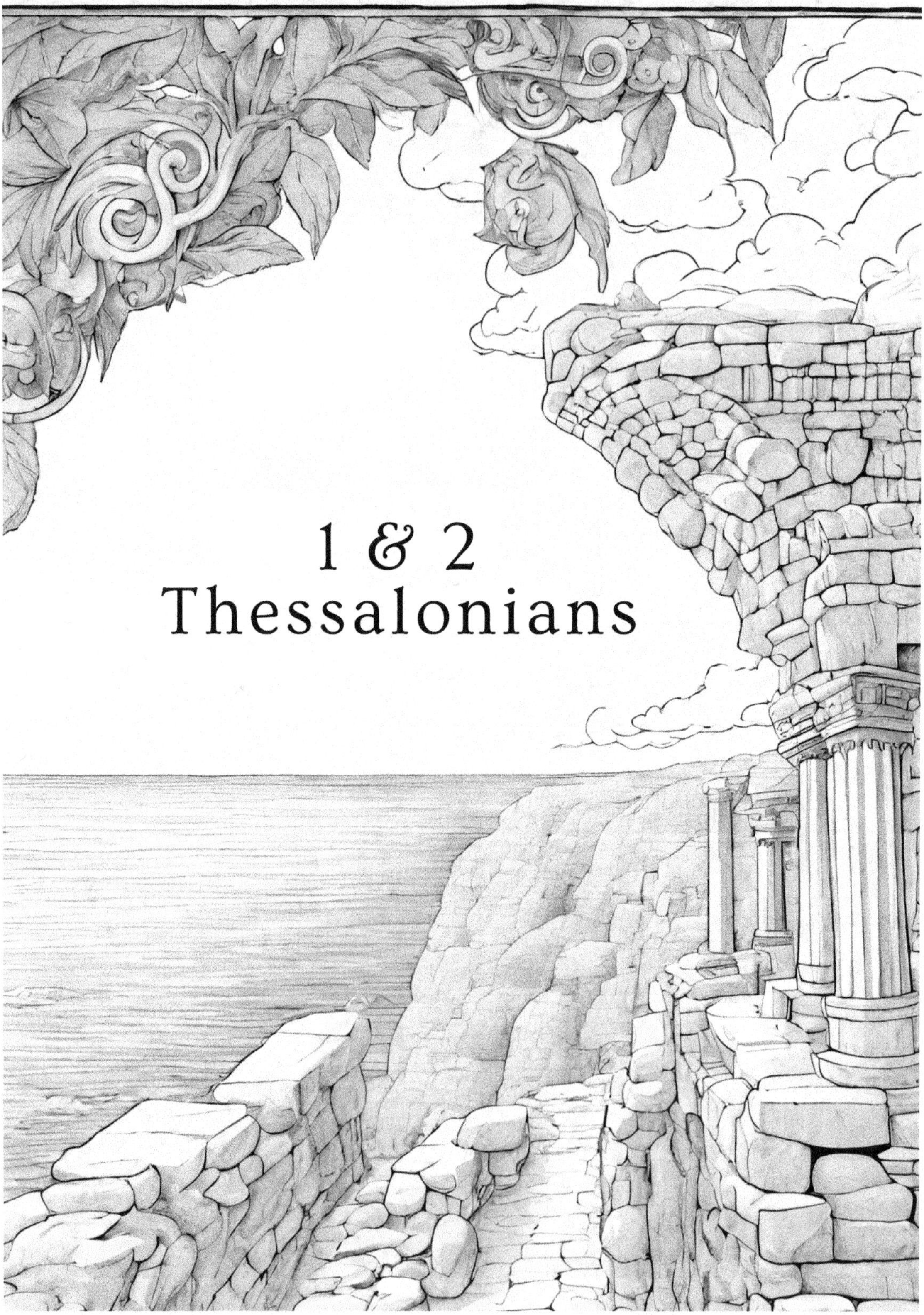

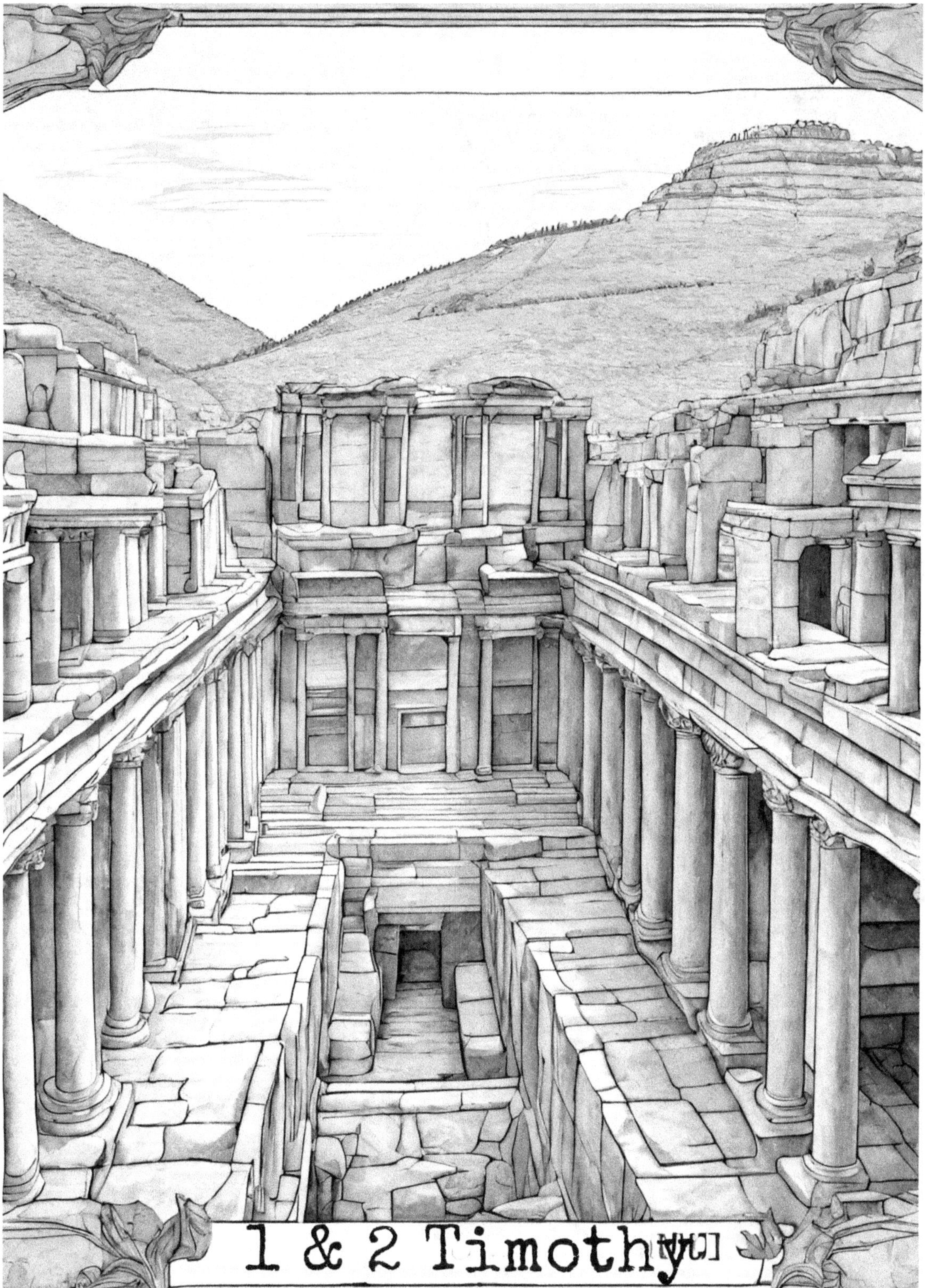

1 & 2 Timothy

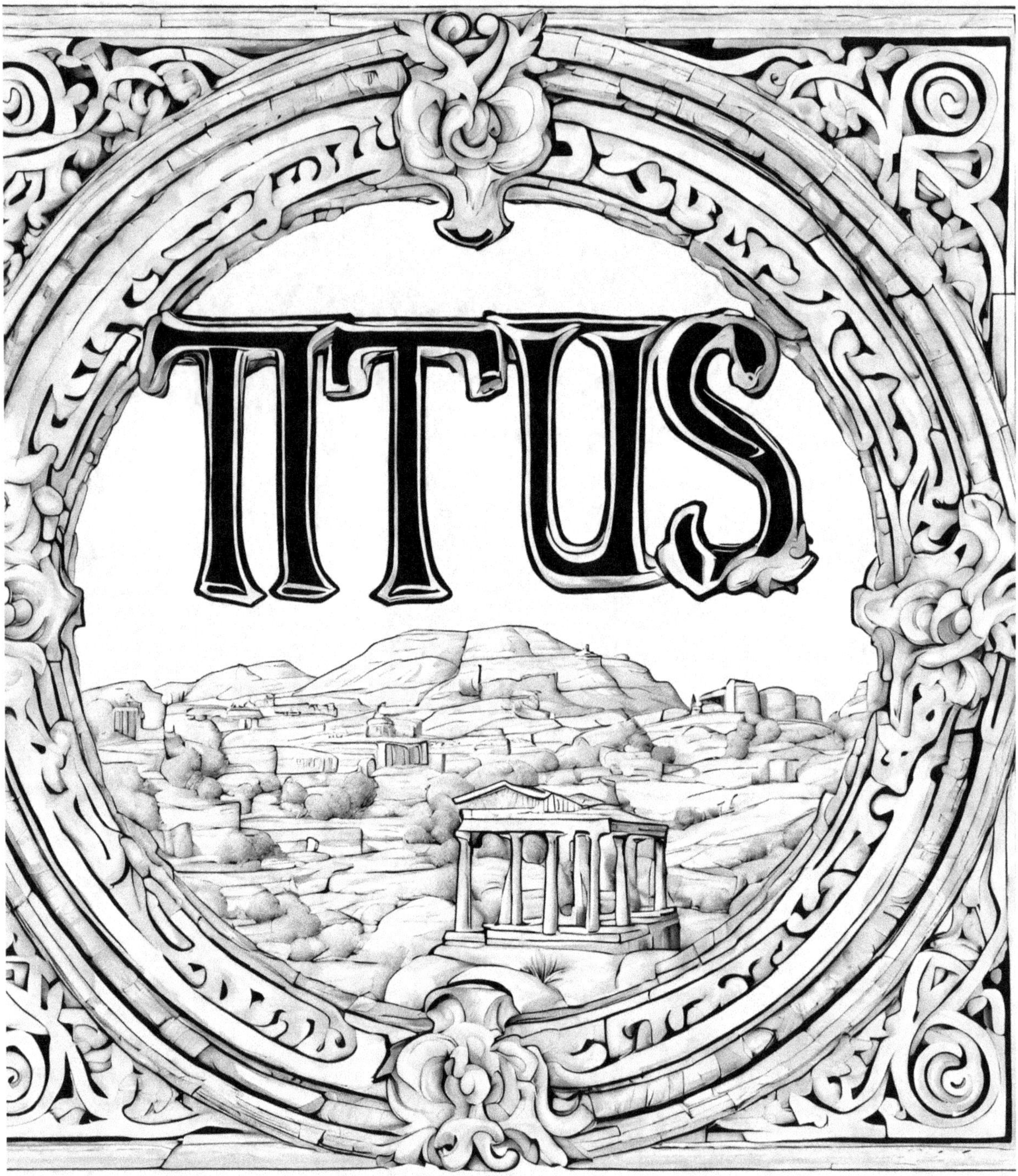
TITUS

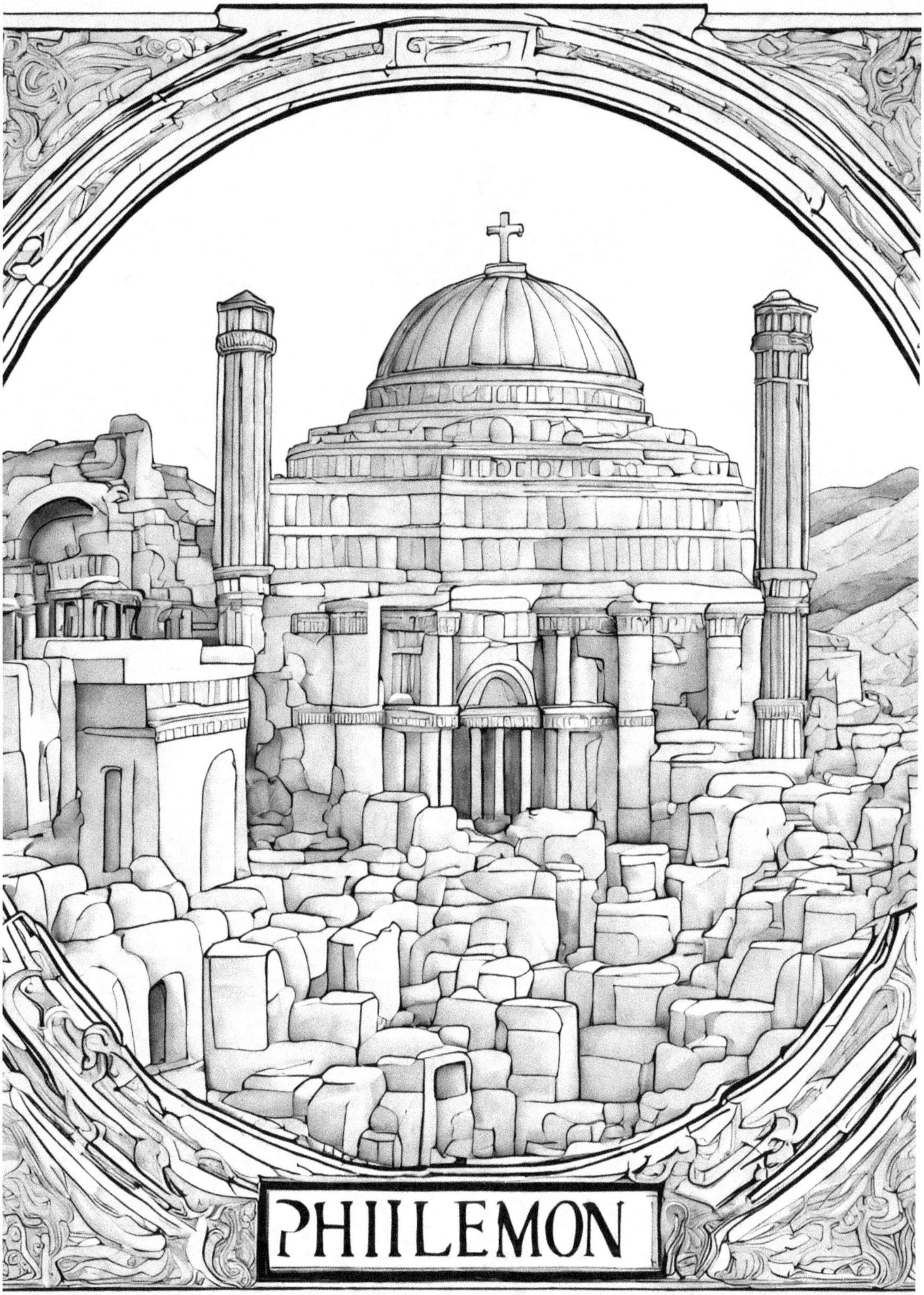
PHILEMON

HEBREWS

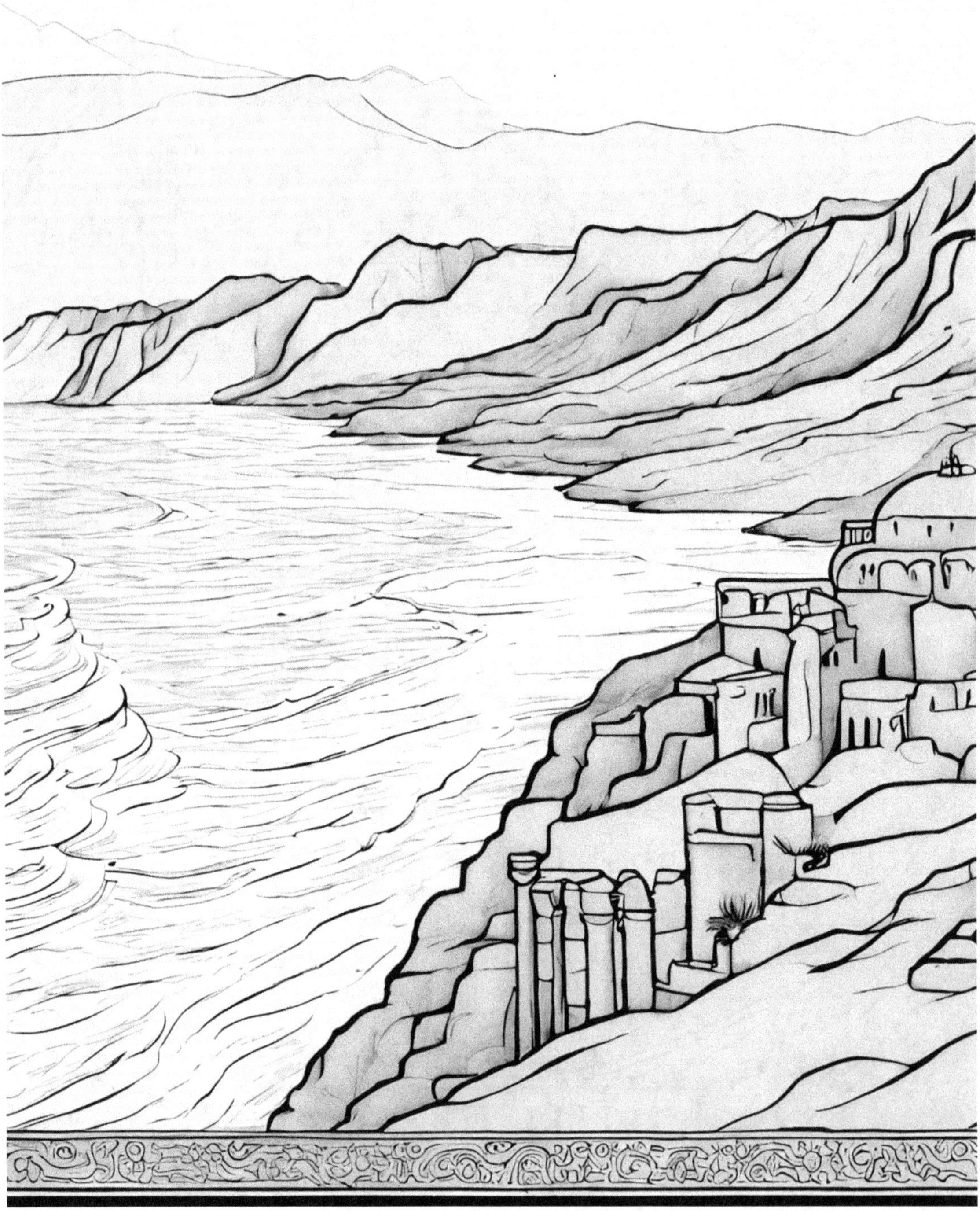

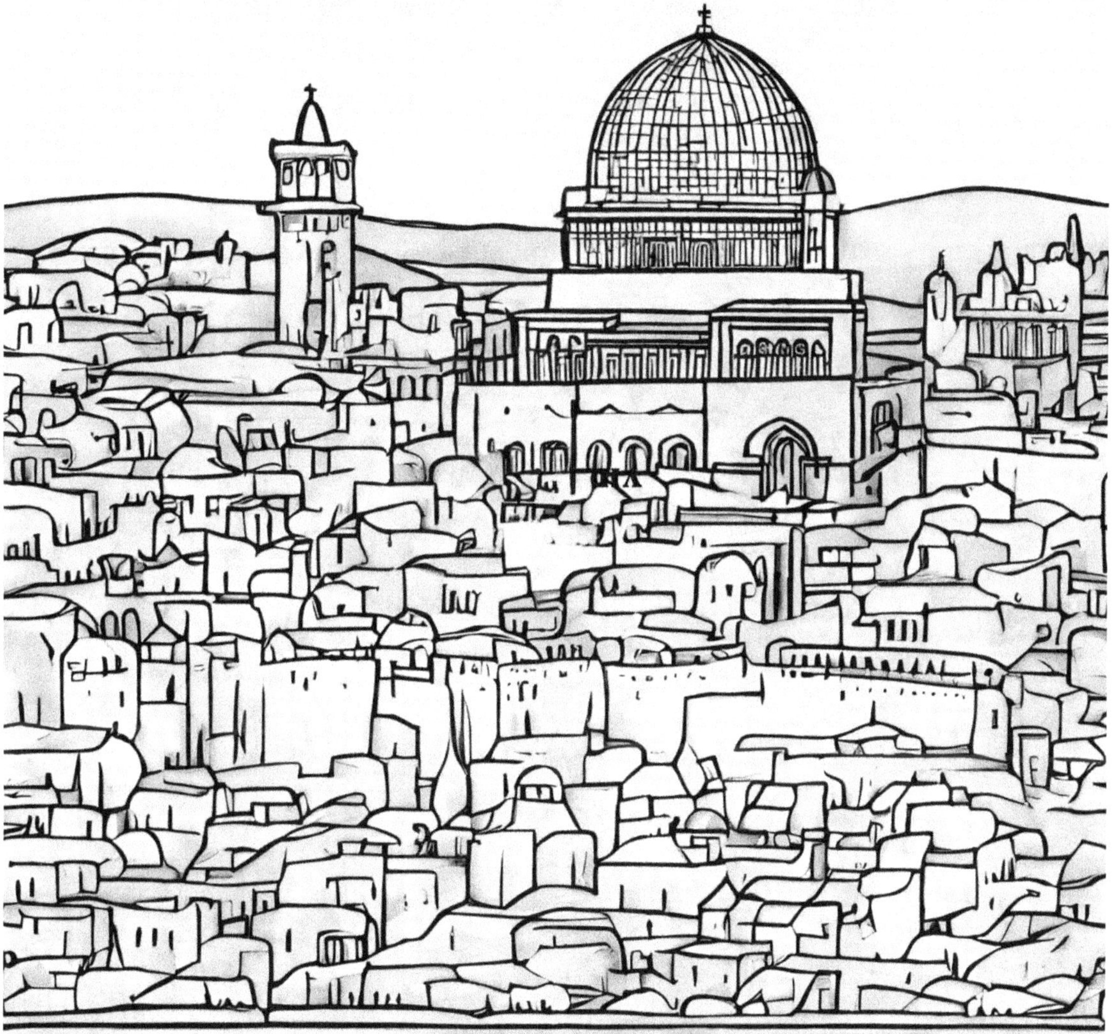

JAMES

1 & 2 Peter

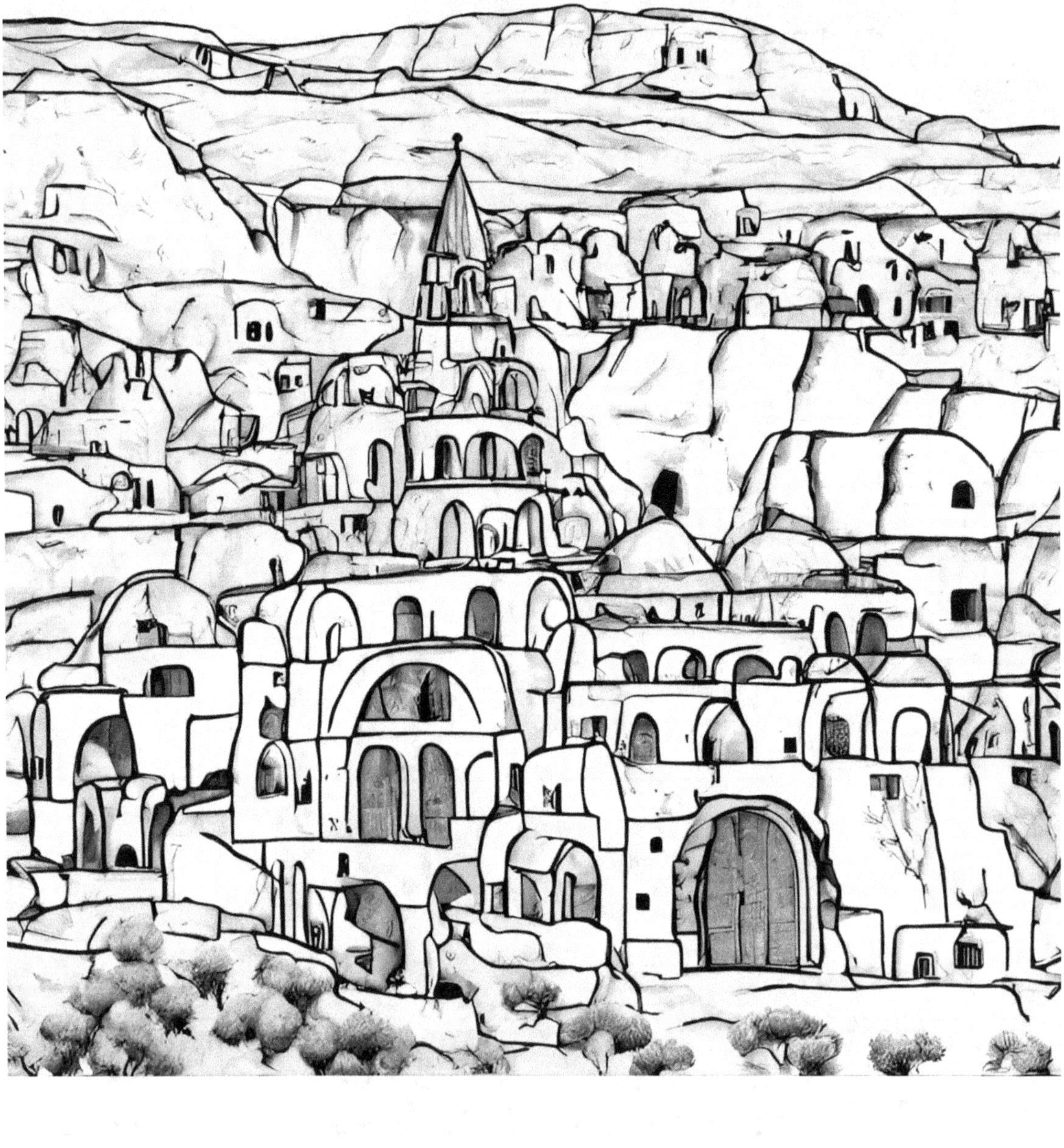

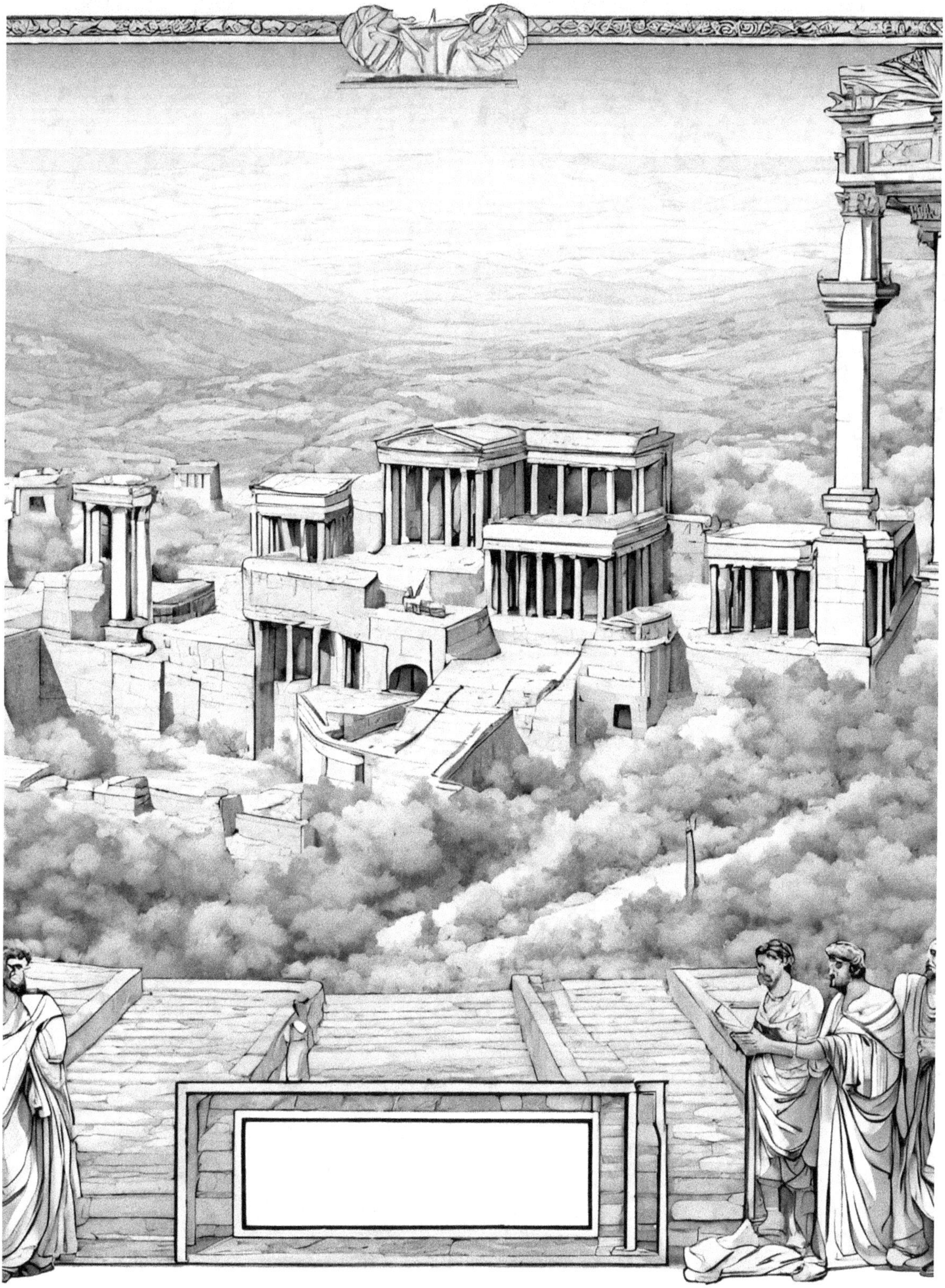

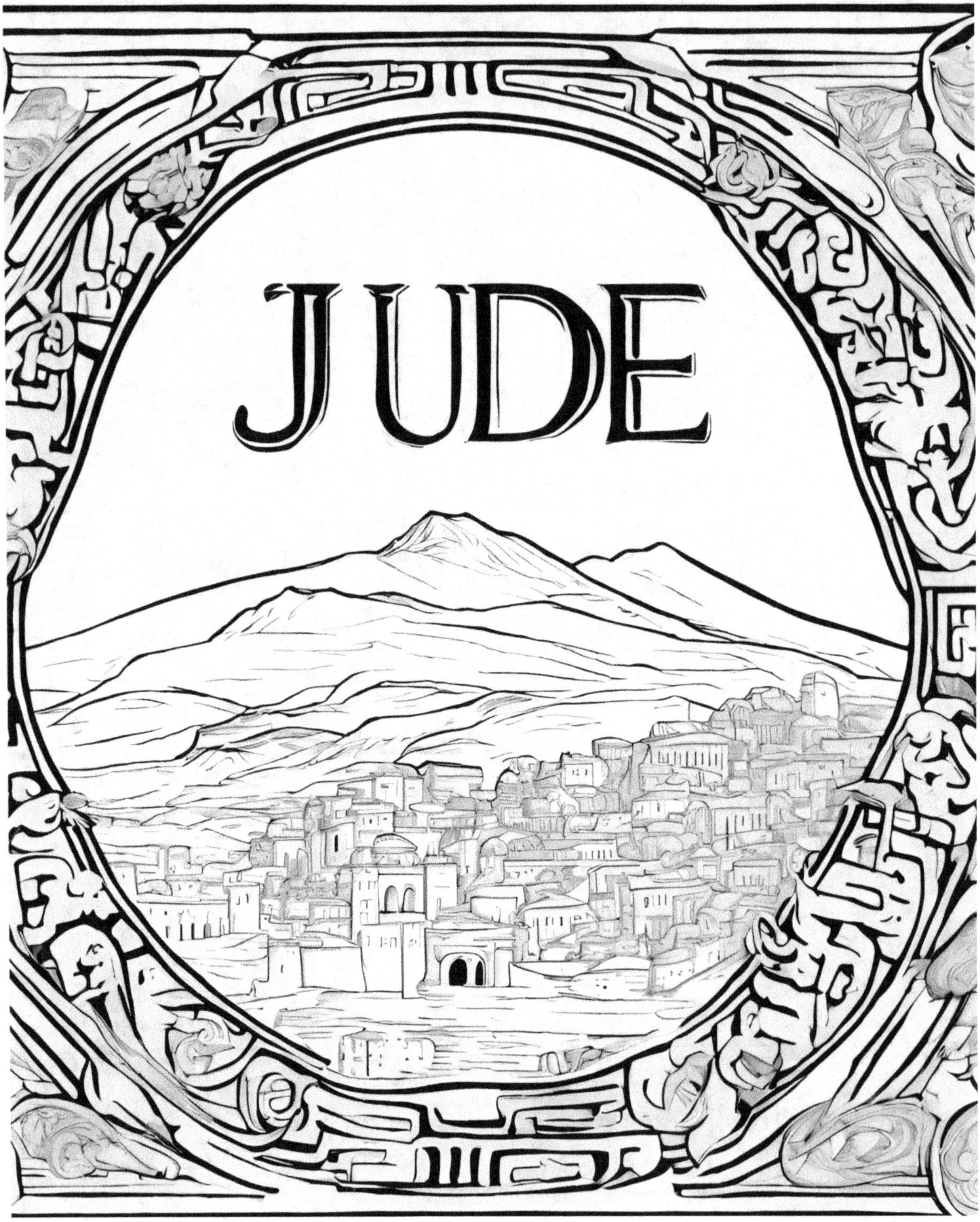
JUDE

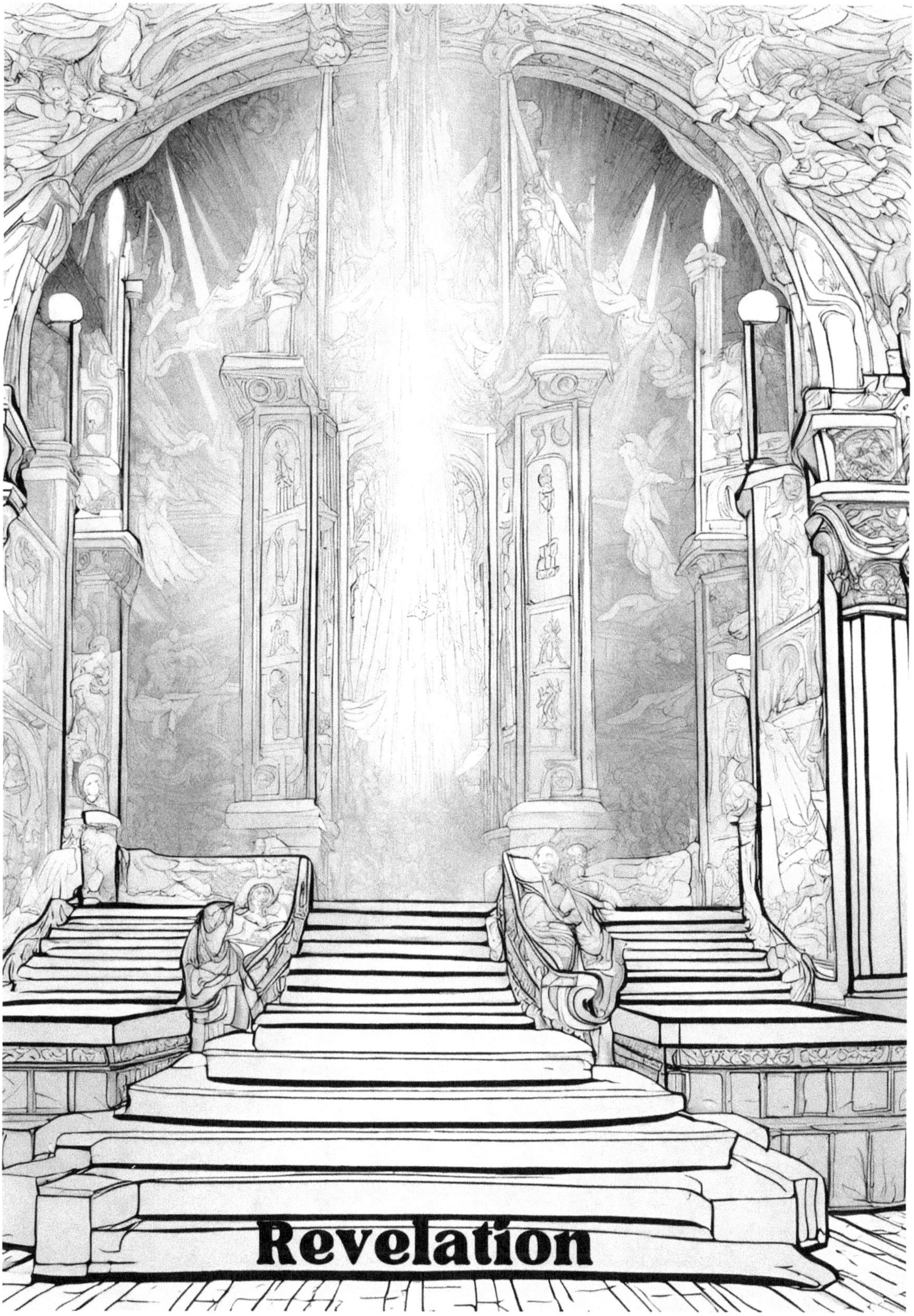
Revelation